Although the author has made every effort to ensure that the information in this book was correct at the time of print, the author does not assume and hereby disclaim any liability to any party for any loss, damage, or disruption caused by errors or omissions, whether such errors or omissions result from negligence, accident, or any other cause.

This book is a memoir. It reflects the author's recollections of her experiences. Some names and characteristics may have been changed or withheld, and some events may have been compressed. This is a book of memories; I have done my best to make it a truthful account of my childhood.

© 2024 Debra Hotton All Rights Reserved.

Second Edition

No part of this book may be reproduced or transmitted in any form or by any means, electronic or mechanical, including photocopying or recording, or by any information storage and retrieval system, without permission in writing from the publisher.

In My Mother's Shadow

by
Debby Hotton

I would like to dedicate this book to my children, Shayne, Taryn and Shaniya-rae, so that they may know what my life was like before they entered the world. In particular, Taryn for helping me to write this book as I shed so many tears and had to relive so many memories.

Introduction

I learned at a very young age that bad things happen to good people.

Physical scars heal quickly but emotional ones are there forever. They sit festering inside you and present themselves in unimaginable ways. We just have to find a way to close the chapter somehow and go on with our life.

I feel I am forever living in the shadow of the cruel words and actions that I suffered when I was growing up. They ring in my head on a daily basis as if entombed in my very being.

Our memories are what define us.

As I sit on a park bench watching the children laughing and playing so carefree, I think of how I was robbed of my childhood. It may sound strange but at the age of 64, I still feel like there's a child inside of me waiting to grow up, like a rosebud waiting to bloom into a rose.

I was born in 1956 to a schizophrenic, bi-polar mother, and a father who died too young as the result of an accident when I was just seven years old.

The earliest recollection I have of my mother was when I was three years old. Dad and I drove up the long drive to the Ashburn Hall: Lunatic Asylum. Mum came walking towards the car with the nurse. She leaned in the car window, looked at me in the back seat, then looked at Dad.

"Who's that little girl?"

My mother was in and out of psychiatric hospitals for most of her life being treated for anxiety, depression, and hallucinations. During these admissions she received electroconvulsive therapy.

I was eight years old when I first thought about running away.

This is my story.

Mum's Early Years

Born in 1916 to Edwin—and Florence, a homemaker, my mother Hazel Elsie Bell, was one of five children - three girls and two boys.

(Mum as a toddler)

Edwin was born in Newcastle, Australia, but was married in New Zealand.

(Edwin and Florence's wedding photo)

Edwin graduated with his psychiatric diploma on 31 March 1919.

Edwin was tall, and stern. He had dark hair and was thick set, without being overweight. He was a hard man and was physically abusive to all of his children. My mother recounted many incidents where her brothers had misbehaved, and her father struck them over the head with a plank of wood. Mum never recounted seeing any abuse toward her mother, so whether Edwin was violent towards Florence remains unknown, but given her timid nature, it seems likely.

Florence was tall and thin - six feet to be precise. My grandmother was described by my mother as a timid, quiet, gentle person who suffered from anxiety throughout her life.

(My Grandfather Edwin)

(The last photo taken of my grandmother before she passed away)

Mum was the youngest daughter and was the second youngest child in her family. She was raised in a strictly Brethren household. On a Sunday morning, all of the children were dressed in their Sunday best and taken to church - the girls with hats, and the boys without, lest any females enter the church without their head covered. Children remained in the service with their parents, but there was a Bible class held for teenagers on a Sunday night. After church, the family would go home, have lunch and spend the afternoon on their knees in prayer. If mum got up for any reason, her father would hit her over the head with a Bible. If a Bible was not available, he used his shoe.

During the week, strict rules were in place which ensured that the children would be kept pure. No jewellery or makeup was to be worn and women were not allowed to cut their hair, since a woman's hair was her 'crowning glory'. Each night before bed, my grandfather would read a selection of scriptures before the children would all pray for forgiveness for being so 'sinful' during the day. As adults, children were encouraged to choose to be baptised, a sign of their own commitment to the faith. At 18, mum chose to be baptised and was welcomed into the church as an adult member.

From the age of five, Mum attended school with her brothers and sisters.

Seacliff Mental Hospital

As a child, Mum's Father was employed at the Seacliff Mental Hospital. She was consequently raised on the grounds, and it is my belief that this early start impacted her own mental health.

Situated about 30 kilometres north of Dunedin, Seacliff Lunatic Asylum was once a thriving psychiatric hospital. The asylum at Seacliff was world class for its rehabilitative model of mental health treatment. The grounds included not only grand buildings but orchards, gardens and greenhouses. These idyllic grounds were thought to be part of a holistic approach to mental wellness, partly due to the philosophy of Truby King, who was appointed superintendent of Seacliff, and who pioneered new forms of treatment including nutritious diets, fresh air and exercise and working programs for patients.

At the time it was built, Seacliff was the largest building in New Zealand, with enough room to house 500 patients, and 50 staff on the grounds. Mum's father was one such staff member who was housed on the grounds. From a young age, my mother lived on the grounds in one of several small cottages provided free for staff. By the time Mum lived there, the facility had been renamed to Seacliff Mental Hospital. Mum attended Seacliff school from the age of five, starting in 1921. Mum shared many stories with me about her experience living on the grounds. One story in particular sent tingles down my spine.

Lionel Terry was a white supremacist who had paranoid schizophrenia. This often-included messianic religious delusions, similar to what my mother would later experience. He was known for being dangerous, mainly due to his obsession with racial segregation, and passionate hatred for 'black and coloured races', especially the Chinese. He came into the care of the facility after having committed a hate crime when he shot and killed Chinese Immigrant Joe Kum Yung in 1905. After initially being sentenced to death, his appeal won him a reduced sentence to life in a psychiatric institution, due to insanity. After having been placed in Christchurch's Sunnyside Asylum (from which he escaped twice), he was sent to be treated at Seacliff under the care of my grandfather, Edwin Bell.

    At Seacliff, Terry was kept in solitary confinement, and his condition appeared to be improving. He gradually earned freedoms such as painting, keeping pets, and gardening, before suffering a deterioration in his mental state and assaulting a doctor who was attempting to administer a typhoid vaccination on him. He had escaped from Seacliff twice before my mother's time and left the premises. One of his escapes, where he didn't make it quite so far, took place during my mother's time at Seacliff, and in later years, she could recall it vividly.

    In the thick of winter, early one evening, Lionel escaped the walls of the asylum, and a manhunt began throughout the staff village. With snow coming down heavily in blizzard conditions, the search was postponed until early the next morning. When the village awoke the next morning, Lionel was still at large, but the snow had not been able to conceal his presence at my mother's house. When my grandmother opened her front door, Lionel's footprints led from the front door of the cottage, along to my mother's bedroom window and away into the trees where he continued to run. He was apprehended the following night in the forest surrounding the asylum.

During her childhood at Seacliff, my mother was exposed to many disturbing incidents, with one recurring one in particular that she often spoke of. A patient that nicknamed himself 'Cow Man', who was convinced that he was a cow, frequently peered through my mother's fence which bordered the asylum grounds. With his hair shaved into the shape of two horns, his appearance frightened her, but not as much as the loud, low moo-ing that he directed at her, which sent her running home to her mother in tears.

Seacliff's history continued, housing one of New Zealand's most famous writers Janet Frame, and ward five being burned to the ground in a fire in 1942, that took the lives of 37 patients. At the time, this was New Zealand's worst loss of life, from a single event.

After her father died from tuberculosis he contracted from a patient at the hospital, my grandmother received a few pounds as a bereavement payment. This allowed her to purchase a modest cottage in the Dunedin city area. My mother's siblings and her mother moved to South Dunedin where she remained until she married my father.

Being raised on the grounds of such an institution would later have an irreparable impact on her mental health. It seems natural to think that the environment in which Mum's early life took place, may have normalised the idea of institutional life, and I wonder if this helped her to accept her own placements in mental health facilities as an adult.

Leslie Bell

After the move to South Dunedin, Mum's younger brother Leslie enlisted for World War II service, as a Flight Sergeant in the 83 Bomber Squadron in the Royal New Zealand Air Force.

Prior to Leslie's service, he was hired as a fitter/mechanic for the Public Works Department. He was a member of the Radio Amateur Hobbies Club, where he would build his own shortwave radios.

He also enjoyed making model planes and rode a motorbike.

Leslie was tall and thin—six foot one—and had brown hair. He left on the vessel Awatea, and trained in bombing, gunnery, air observation, air navigation in Canada, before being deployed in Europe. His RNZAF number was NZ405364, rank 'SGT.obs'. For his service, he earned 13 shillings a day.

When Leslie left for service, he left his long-term girlfriend. On a trip home for leave, he asked Joan to marry him, and returned to war, an engaged man.

Sadly, Leslie was shot down over Germany on the 17th of September, 1942, at the age of 23. He was part of a crew of seven soldiers. Leslie was initially considered missing but was later reclassified as 'Killed in Action'. The local paper printed Leslie's picture, with a comment that he was considered missing.

Sergeant-Navigator L. E. Bell, of Dunedin, missing on operations.

His remains were interred at Reichswald Forest War Cemetery, Kleve, Nordrhein-Westfalen, Germany. Joan never married.

(My Uncle Leslie: middle row, fourth from right)

Mum later told me that she was "glad he died," as he had teased her. Most little brothers tease their older sisters, so it's not unusual, but she decided it was emotional abuse.

Kiss in the Dark

After the move, Mum was transferred from the local Seacliff school to Forbury School, which she left in 1929.

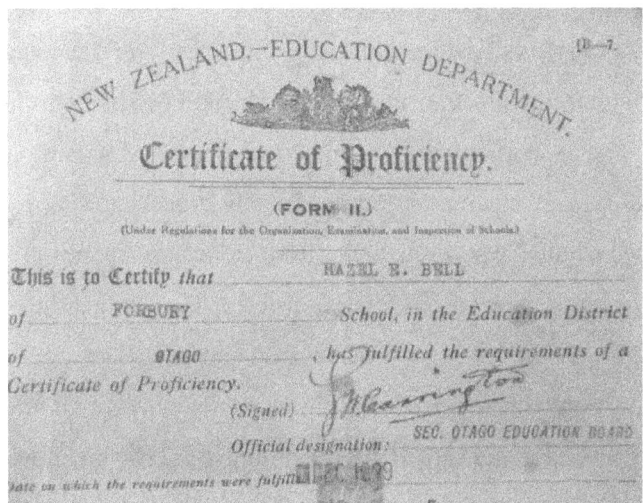

When she was 13 she went to King Edward Technical College in Stuart St to complete secondary school. She only stayed one year.

Mum had anxiety from a young age. This crept from her childhood into her adolescence, and Mum increasingly struggled with being separated from her mother. When she was young, before she was a wife and a mother, Mum seemed to be able to manage her mental health. At 19, Mum still lived at home in South Dunedin with her mother, now a widow. Mum's relationship with her mother was extremely close, closer than that of the other children. As she got older, she found that if she didn't see her mother every day, she became anxious.

When she was 14 her mother asked her to leave school and get a job so that she could contribute to the family income. Fresh out of school, Mum worked in a milk bar until the manager was diagnosed with stomach cancer and sold up. Mum was just a young teenager when she took a full-time job at 'Mrs. Fenton's Cakes,' serving customers. While she was at the cake shop, Mum attended a dance where she met a fresh Policeman recruit in his early twenties. They dated briefly until she decided that the relationship was moving too fast and ended things.

Mum was not particularly tall and had vibrant Hazel eyes, which she was named after. Her hair was brown and was wavy. Her ivory complexion was without blemish and was the envy of people at church. Someone one Sunday commented on the silken quality of her skin, and it was even noted at her funeral that her skin was like a 'movie star'. Mum had a thin frame, but in later years battled with her weight. People often commented on how pretty Mum was, even as she got older.

(Mum, aged 19)

Mum used to attend the dances every Saturday with her girlfriends. Joe Brown's Town Hall Dances were established in 1936 and ran for 30 years. Initially they were held in the concert chamber of Dunedin Town Hall, but as they gained popularity, they were moved to the main town hall. So many people met their husbands and wives at these dances that it was practically a marriage market for young single people in Dunedin.

One Saturday night she went with her best friend, where they met up with another girl that used to attend when they went as a group. This girl had come with a date, Alman Constable (his friends and relations called him Ab). Alman was 5 foot 6 inches, He had unusually pale blue eyes which were often described as 'ice blue' and a button nose.

In his mid 20s, he was already starting to experience thinning hair, though he still had a head of fair hair. A lot of the girls at the dances were interested in him and being picked by him to dance was considered a privilege. Luckily for the other single girls, Dad had an identical twin.

During the night, nobody asked Mum to dance - the number of women at the dances always far outweighed that of the men and it was not appropriate to ask the men to dance, so Mum spent most of the night sitting, enjoying the free refreshments. Spending the night this way wasn't uncommon for Mum and by her own admission she preferred to, since she enjoyed spending time with her girlfriends and chatting. The girl who had arrived with Alman had left early with her friends after she realised that the two of them did not have any chemistry. Alman stayed, enjoying the rest of his evening. At the end of the night, he approached Mum and asked if he could walk her home. Mum was hesitant because he had come with another girl, but he reassured her that this relationship was not going anywhere.

They walked slowly home, stretching the ten-minute walk out. When they reached two gates away from Mum's house, Alman picked a flower from a bush that was leaning out of someone's garden onto the footpath, and asked Mum if she knew what the flower was called, grinning. Mum, suspecting this was just a line, said she didn't know, when he declared that it was called 'Kiss in the Dark." She said goodnight at the gate and went inside. He had promised to come and visit her another time. When she got inside, she showed her mother the flower and asked what it was called. Her mother replied, "Kiss in the Dark."

Life Before Me

Every Saturday night, Mum and Dad would attend the South Dunedin Town Hall dances, and dance together all night. Mum used to get anxious about leaving her mother and the safety of her home at night, to attend the dances. Since she worked during the day, nights were the only free times to spend with my father, so she went nervously.

Things got serious very quickly, and within a few weeks they were engaged to be married. Mum and Dad celebrated their engagement by getting a professional photo taken.

During the engagement, Mum found herself pregnant with my sister, June. In light of her strict Brethren upbringing, a marriage was hurriedly arranged, and took place at the registry office. Mum was concerned about what her mother would say about her pregnancy, and about her giving birth to what would have been considered an illegitimate child. Being pregnant before marriage would have brought shame upon a brethren family, and would certainly not have been considered a Christian way of living.

After the wedding, Dad moved into Mum's parental home in 3 Largo ave with her, where they lived for some time. Dad was unemployed because New Zealand was in the thick of

The Great Depression of the 1930s, and the only way to survive was to share expenses. It was common at this time for families to move in together to make ends meet, and my parents were no exception.

On May 31st, of 1936, June was born, and Mum was soon pregnant with another child due to the lack of contraception available. The only contraceptive product available was a thick rubber condom which was washable and reusable. Most men weren't too fussed on using these as they couldn't feel much.

After June's birth Mum began having panic attacks which furthered her anxiety. Unfortunately, panic attacks weren't recognised or understood as well as they are now, and little help or support was available to help manage them.

On December 4th of 1938, when Mum was still living at Largo Ave with her mother, a severe flood hit, and friends of the family were drowned.

(From left to right; Mum, Daisy, Phyllis)

Following this, Mum often spoke of her mother's anxiety turns and post-traumatic stress disorder, which never quite resolved. Later when Mum lived with her mother as an adult, she recalled her mother suffering from night terrors, calling out "get the children up the hill!" in her sleep. Her mother also lived through the 1918 influenza pandemic, which I'm sure contributed to her anxiety. Given what I know about my grandmother's ongoing anxiety, it isn't surprising that Mum struggled with her own after June's birth.

During the time in which June was a baby, food was rationed and was only attained using food stamps. These were posted out from the New Zealand government to families once a week, and often got stolen from letterboxes. Several times, Mum went to get hers from the post box only to find them missing, so my grandmother opted to pick them up from the local post office in person. Food stamps allowed you to visit the grocer and the butcher where you would exchange them for small amounts of flour, sugar, butter and eggs and a lamb shank. You also got a piece of lard—also known as dripping—which was grated and used in baking and as a spread for sandwiches. This had to last the week and to go around the whole family. Due to the lack of food, a lot of men began going down to the wharf when shipments were due and rocking the trucks until they overturned, and the food fell out. These 'snatch and grab' raids were illegal, and dangerous, but many men, including my father, were prepared to risk going to jail to feed their families.

Out of necessity, Dad quickly learned to be a vegetable gardener, something which he remained fond of throughout his life. There was no fresh produce available unless you grew your own. When the rations ran out, my mother and grandmother would make 'war soup' using a pot of water and any available vegetables. After it was used for a meal, it remained on the coal range. The next day more water would be added to it, and it was brought back to the boil to make it go further, for another meal. My grandmother was six feet tall and extremely thin. The first time I saw a photo of her I asked my mother why she was so thin. Mum told me that when there wasn't much food for a meal, her mother used to decline to eat, saying that she wasn't feeling hungry and that Mum who was breastfeeding, and the grandchildren, needed it more.

(From left to right, Mum's sister Daisy, Mum and her Mother Florence)

(Mum, with her Mum, Florence)

When the depression ended, Dad was able to find some work, and the family moved into a one-bedroom flat in Royal Terrace.

By this time the Second World War was in full swing, and men were getting drafted. My three brothers had also joined the family. Brian was born on December 23rd, 1937. Eddie followed on April 9th, 1939, and Alec on 3rd November 1940.

Because Dad had a large family, he was not drafted into the war in the early stages. During the depression, while he was unemployed, Dad undertook some free training with St John's Ambulance as a paramedic. In 1941 Dad was called to the war, not as a soldier, but as a medic as Private #492608 in the New Zealand Army. This left my mother alone, with four children under five.

(Dad on the right)

By the time my father joined the New Zealand Army, they had four children. After he left, Mum used to walk from her flat to her mother's house in South Dunedin with her youngest in the pram and three walking by her side. Mum made the decision to move back into the two-bedroom cottage with her mother and her children for financial reasons and for support. Mum knew that she would not cope with 4 children on her own. By this stage my grandmother was not able to work as her health was preventing her from holding down a job, so this also helped out with expenses. While she was living there, June and Brian started at Forbury School, followed by Eddie and Alec. When Dad came back from the war, he moved into the house with them so that they could get back on their feet. Dad picked up work first at the Dunedin Gasworks, and later as a tram-driver, and they were able to once again get a place of their own.

(Dad in his Tram uniform)

During his time at the Gasworks, Dad used to be approached by people with cats who wanted them gassed. He was often handed sacks with cats in them (sometimes multiple), and paid cash to throw them into the gas and 'dispose' of them. Dad instead would take the cats, and the cash, and bring the cats' home. This happened frequently, and so our home quickly became full of them. At one stage, we had accrued around 30. I loved it because I have been a 'Crazy Cat Lady' since infancy.

My older brothers and sister had a different upbringing to mine. They were raised in a two-parent household with the additional support from my grandmother, and benefited from a two-income family, as my father made sufficient money to support us, and mum chose to work part-time when the kids were at school.

(Mum and Dad walking along town)

In 1944, Mum had a nervous breakdown and went to Queen Mary Hospital in Hanmer Springs for seven months. Like Seacliff Mental Hospital, the premises was set amongst 40 acres of landscaped grounds, and was initially used as a convalescent home for soldiers who were suffering from 'Shell Shock' (now known as Post Traumatic Stress Disorder) after World War I. Following this period, it became a treatment centre for people with 'nervous disorders', including alcohol and drug addictions. The property contained three buildings which were constructed in the 1900s, and although it closed in 2003, it remains a historical site of significance according to Heritage New Zealand.

Mum's departure left Dad to cope with the children on his own. My sister June was 8, my brother Brian was 7, Eddie was 5. and Alec was 4. This must have been very difficult for him and I'm not sure how he managed to work. He must have engaged the help of my grandmother, as because it was a private hospital, he would have had to pay for Mum's care. Mum had a history of nervous breakdowns but the most she had ever away been 3 months at a time. Mum told me she loved it there and didn't want to come home, back to the responsibilities of daily life. She said my father came up and discharged her and told her she was needed at home, so he put her suitcases in the car and drove her back. I think this is where she developed her unhealthy obsession with nurses and doctors, as the patients socialised with them on their days off, she took a particular liking to a young nurse named Christine from

Scotland and often caddied for during a golf game on the course on the grounds.

(Mum and nurse, Christine)

(Hanmer Springs nurses when Mum was there)

(Mum at Hanmer Springs)

(Hanmer Springs Hospital in the 1940's)

Mum and Dad were foster parents to children needing short-term care, most of which were taken in by my parents before I was alive. When my siblings were teenagers, Dad's brother and his wife went on a drinking bender for three days. A neighbour alerted the local child welfare office that the children had been left at home alone and the five children were uplifted into state care. Mum and Dad were asked to care for the youngest two. The youngest child was a little boy no older than one year of age. When he first arrived, Mum said the baby smelled strongly of vomit and faeces, so Mum took him into the bathroom to bathe him. When she went to undress him for this wash, she couldn't remove his singlet because he had been wearing it so long that the fabric had adhered to his skin. Mum had to soak him in the bath until the singlet would ease itself off his body. He also suffered from severe nappy rash. She later found out that the older siblings had been giving the baby bottles in the cot but had not been changing his nappy. The kids were adopted out separately in the end, the baby remained with Mum for a long time but was eventually adopted out.

Mum and Dad went on to take multiple placements, 28 in total. These included a newborn baby, Maureen. Maureen was the last foster child that was parented by both Mum and Dad. Maureen's mother lived in Corstorphine and had been struggling with alcoholism, as well as creating an environment at home that wasn't suitable for children. She had other children which had all been placed in foster homes.

Maureen was just an infant when I was born. Mum always said that having Maureen in the house was the reason she got pregnant, caring for a baby. Maureen had blonde curls and a pale complexion and could have been my natural sister. We grew up together and were often mistaken for sisters because of the similarity in our ages and our physical appearance. Mum often told me that Maureen was not my sister, and that there was a good chance she would be going home again. She was almost five years old when she did. Social Welfare (now known as Oranga Tamariki) returned Maureen to her mother after deciding that she was now fit to parent her. Mum and Dad were upset, as they had hoped to adopt Maureen, and I grieved for the sister that

I could have had. I've often thought over the years how much better my life would have been if I hadn't ended up being alone with Mum for the rest of my childhood.

(Maureen and I)

I was the first in my family to not be born at home. When Mum was pregnant with me it was becoming a trend that babies should be born in the maternity home. She later said she regretted this, as I contracted the "H-bug" which was in the maternity home at the time. I became very unwell soon after the birth, and it wasn't clear if I would survive. A complication of the H-bug also left me with an infection in my navel, which required surgery. Because I was so unwell, Mum was incredibly tired, and I think this contributed to her mental deterioration at that time.

Alec came in to visit one afternoon and found Mum holding me down under the water, while bathing me in the kitchen sink. Alec ran to the sink and grabbed me, wrapping a towel around me, and called an ambulance. Luckily, she had just started holding me under the water when he walked in, so I recovered, and when the ambulance got there, they called the police. Alec recounted this story multiple times over the years. He often said that if he hadn't come home when he did, that I wouldn't be alive. Dad admitted Mum back into psychiatric care and took over the care of me himself.

There are no photos of me before I was about nine months old, a fact which I attribute to the time that Mum was away receiving care, and Dad juggled everything at home. We still had our foster daughter Maureen at the time, and Dad would have had to continue to work to keep up financially. He had a lot on his plate during this time.

Family Life

During my first years, when Dad was alive, I was sheltered from Mum's deteriorating mental illness.

Since I lost my father at a young age, I don't know much about his years before he met my mother. However, in recent years, I have been able to find out some interesting information online, from ancestry records. Dad was born on the 18th of October 1911 and raised in Dunedin. His mother Elizabeth Jane was New Zealand born to Irish parents, who immigrated to New Zealand after the signing of the Treaty of Waitangi. His Father Henry was of English and Northern Irish descent, having immigrated to New Zealand as well. This made Dad's parents among the first generation of New Zealanders to be born in the South Island.

Dad was part of a large family. He was one of seven - Lyn, Justin, Keith, Fin, Vernon (my father's twin), and Audrey. Dad's mother died of cancer at age 65, and most of his brothers died young, but the most significant death for Dad was his brother Vernon.

(Dad's family: left back Dad, right back Vernon. In the middle is my paternal Grandfather)

(One of Dad and Vernon's school photos. Dad is in the second row on the right at the end, and Vernon is far left in the front row. Approximately 8-9 years of age)

Two years before my father passed away, he woke up screaming early one morning, yelling "something is happening to Vernon!" Mum told him he was having a nightmare, and to go back to sleep. Later that day, there was a phone call saying that Vernon had drowned. As twins, they were so connected that dad could feel Vernon's passing, before he was told about it.

(Vernon with his wife)

Life, for me, was better while Dad was alive. He was my hero and my protector, and I was the apple of his eye, the baby of the family.

The few memories that I have of Dad are of a warm, loving parent. I had three brothers and one sister, with the next child up to me being sixteen years older than me. Having finished with their family, my arrival was a surprise. Dad used to say I was an 'afterthought' while Mum called me a 'mistake'. If I was an afterthought, I seemed to be an afterthought that Dad was quite happy to have. During my growing up years, Mum would later tell me in great detail about the methods she had used, to try and abort me. Knitting needles, douches, gin, baking soda, hot baths—but to her dismay nothing worked. But God wanted me here, so here I am.

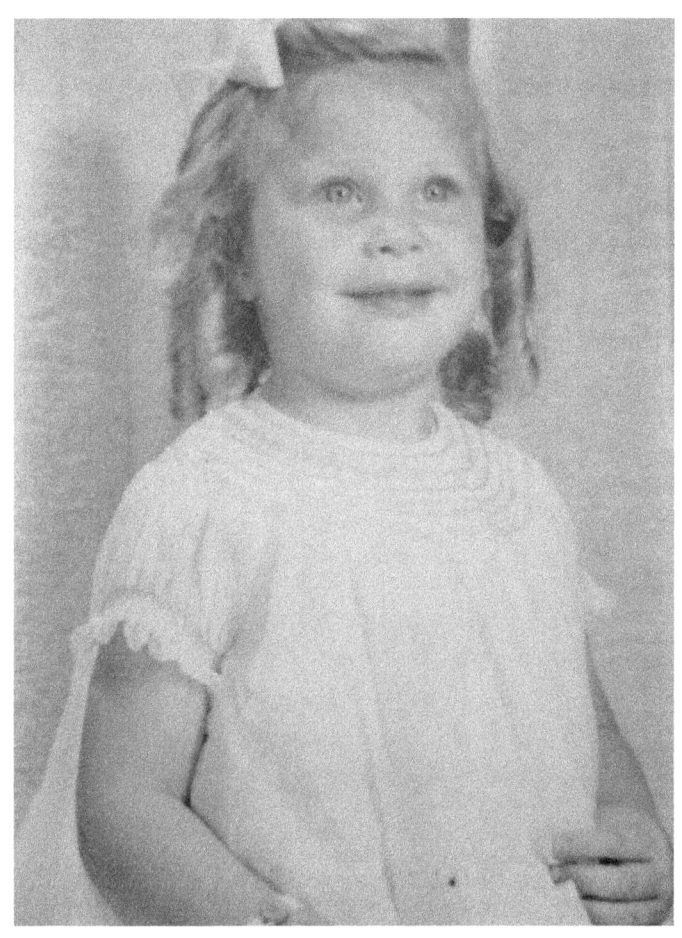

(Me as a baby)

I remember playing 'hairdresser' and putting curlers onto his balding head, and we played 'fish and chip shops'. My father was an excellent customer who regularly ordered a meal of doll clothing, which I 'deep fried' in a wire basket before carefully wrapping in newspaper and handing it to him. I also ran a shop where my father would purchase my toys and pay with play money. Dad would make animals out of wood and paint them up and sell them, he sold many large butterflies for the outside of houses, he also made me a wooden dolls house and bought me an expensive top of the line tricycle.

(The doll's house that Dad made me)

(The tricycle Dad bought me)

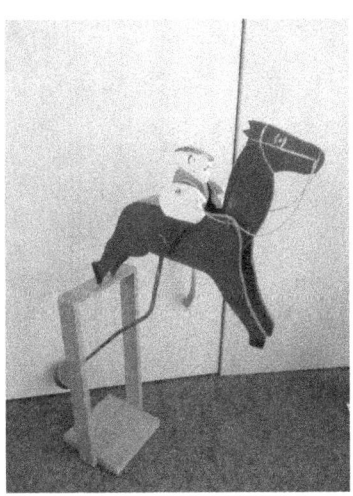

(This is a wee bobbing horse that Dad made me, sadly over the years, the tail has fallen off)

We lived at 20 Begg St, St Kilda when I started school at Columba College. Dad insisted that I attend this private school on the other side of town because I was 'his little princess'.

(Me in my Columba College uniform)

On my first day, Mum went and found Aunty Lorna and Uncle Ralph's daughter Denise Markham and asked if she would check on me at lunchtime. I didn't know anybody at the school, and so when I saw her familiar face, I ran up and hugged her.

(Me with Ralph Markham. This was taken at Denise Markhams's 21st birthday party)

My Aunty Daisy bought me that wee gold mouse brooch when she was on holiday as she knew I loved mice. I still have it.

(Me and Mum)

My first teacher was Ms. Brewster, and after school I had ballet lessons with Shona Dunlop. After only a few weeks of this long commute, Mum and Dad decided it was time to start looking for housing in the area.

Mum never learned to drive so either Dad (if he wasn't away working on the railway) or Alec took me to school. Alec used to take me to school in the morning, and then go to work himself. In his 3pm smoko break he would pick me up and drop me home. It was a hassle for him, but he still lived at home at that stage. When we were going down Pacific st, Alec used to keep pumping the brakes and saying that the car had no brakes. The first few days I fell for it, but after that I didn't.

(My brother Alec and Loraine when they were dating, at our home in Begg st)

Alec got married when I was five, in 1961, and I was asked to be a flower girl. I wore a white nylon dress with a teal blue bow on my head, and I carried a basket of flowers.

At the wedding dance, my dad lifted me onto the piano to sing a song. I only knew hymns and carols. When he asked me what I wanted to sing, I said, *Away in a Manger.* Luckily, the pianist knew it. That was my second public performance. My first was in a school concert while I attended Columba College, where I was dressed in a crinoline dress with a big picture hat and I had to recite *Mary, Mary, Quite Contrary*, "how does your garden grow?". The teacher had asked a couple of other students to do it, and I was the only one who could get my mouth around the words "quite contrary", and I was picked to perform it, and wear the pretty dress. The picture we had taken at Alec's wedding, was the last family photo we had taken while my father was alive. It's the last picture I have of myself with both of my parents.

(Me as flower girl at Alec's wedding)

Our house at Begg St was cosy and comfortable. I have warm memories of the time we lived in this house with Dad, and with my brothers Alec, Eddie, and my sister June. The front yard had an Orange Blossom tree. In exchange for reduced rent, my father renovated the house, painting and wallpapering each room. My bedroom received new ballerina wallpaper and the leftovers were used to cover my books for school. While we were there my father also installed a brand-new kitchen for the landlord, which he built himself.

(Our house at Begg St, as it stands today)

At the Begg St house, Dad and my brothers used to pull cars to bits in the front yard and put them back together, cleaning the pieces and repairing broken motors. Mum always used to complain about the mess. My brothers were popular at the South Dunedin Town Hall dances, drawing the gaze of all the girls. They were tall, good-looking, and wore shirts with a lurex thread in colours of orange, and red, with socks to match, with shiny patent winklepicker shoes. They slicked back their hair with Brylcreem into curls on the top, and a ducktail at the back. It was the 'teddy boy' era, and they fitted in perfectly. My brothers had nicknames for each other. My brother Brian had a big bottom and earned the name "Twenty pants", because in those days the pants were numbered for size using different waist measurements and he wore a size 20. Eddie got his nickname from an incident where he walked into a power pole with his head down, on a walk, earning him the name "Lemon Head". Alec was "Little Wibber" because he was the youngest. Those names stuck into adulthood. Brian would come in the door as an adult, asking if "Little Wibber" was home.

(My brother Brian as a teenager)

(My brother Alec as a teenager)

While we lived at this house, we were close to the beach, so Dad used to take me to the Ocean Beach Railway for fun. The train was established in 1961 and is still located on John Wilson Drive in Dunedin today. It is New Zealand's oldest preservation railway. I remember walking over to the railway with Dad, which would take about 20 minutes, and then walking back home.

At this house, I also had a foxy puppy that I named Fairy. I found her dead in the backyard at a few months old. We buried her in our backyard. Dad said she may have chewed the stick he had been stirring paint with, as paint then contained lead. But Mum's theory was that my brother Brian had bought his big German Shepherd, Salaman, and that Fairy, who was tied to the clothesline, dropped dead at the sight of her. Salaman bit the vet when he came to Brian's house in Tomahawk, to give him a vaccination. He was ordered to be put to sleep. He was a gentle giant. My nieces and nephews, when they were small, used to ride on his back and Brian said that the vet came up behind him and gave him a fright.

(Me with 'Fairy')

When we first moved into the house, my sister June was still living at home. At 21 she was still having to adhere to a

10pm curfew enforced by my mother. By this time, she was dating a boy called John. He was nice looking, and had thick, black hair like Elvis. One night she went out to see John and came home late. When she walked in the front door everything was dark and June was planning on sneaking in and going to bed. Little did she know that when Mum heard her being dropped off and she got on a chair behind the door with a rolling pin in her hand. When June came in Mum hit her on the head with it. Because of this incident, June spoke to John, and they decided that they would get married, and move away together. They had a Registry wedding, and she wore a women's skirt suit.

(My sister June and her husband John)

My oldest brother Brian also had a Registry wedding. He married a full-blooded Maori girl named Mary Paki. She was a descendant of a chief.

My brother Eddie moved out of our family home when he was a teenager to go flatting. When my brother Alec was 21, he got married and moved out and it was just the three of us. Once Alec was gone, my parents decided that they could downsize, and needed to rent a house closer to my school, so we moved to Falcon St, Roslyn. We didn't stay there very long—only a few weeks—because the house was damp. After that, Mum and Dad found a new rental at 703 Highgate, Maori Hill. We moved into the Highgate house when I was 6 years old. I remember riding my tricycle up and down the footpath outside while Dad set up the beds on our first night in the house.

I have very little memory of our time at this house. It was a small home, a semi-villa painted moss-green, like many of the houses were at that time. In the living room, Mum wallpapered the panel above the fireplace with wallpaper that had river stones patterned on it. The cereal we used to buy used to come with little plastic lizards which Mum nailed up on the wallpaper panel, in the crevices between the rocks. I remember staring up at this, fascinated with all of the lizards we had collected.

This is the house we were living in when Dad had his accident at work.

(703 Highgate, as it stands today)

Life With Dad

Dad had taken work as a carpenter, working on the New Zealand Railways, which was controlled by the Public Works Department. By the 1950s, there were more than 1300 railway stations in New Zealand, and rail travel was the predominant means of moving around. Railway stations were busy places, and many had refreshment rooms. The refreshment rooms had their own Crown Lynn china with an NZR logo on each piece.

Sometimes Mum and I would go down to the Railway Station for a cup of tea and a cake. We weren't travelling, we just enjoyed the food and the atmosphere.

Dad's job at the Railway consisted of repairing the railway sleepers on the tracks, maintaining the worker's huts, completing wood repairs on the cabs, and other odd jobs.

In the 1950s and 1960s this job was remote, and the workers lived in modified train carriages while they were on the job, including Dad. The carriages had the seats removed, and bunks installed for sleeping. They also came with a coal range for cooking and heating.

The cabs were purposely placed in locations around Central Otago and I stayed in several with my father when mum was in the mental hospital. Because the workers all knew each other, and the cabs were placed so close to the railway line, the train drivers used to toot as they were approaching. From around the age of three, when the train came past, I would run and grab my handkerchief and wave to the driver.

Each caboose came with a pre-built outhouse building. When each worker arrived, he had to dig himself a long drop toilet and place the outhouse over it. It was my job to cut squares of newspaper to put into the long drop to use. When the job was up, the worker had to fill in the hole and leave the outhouse for the next person. I have vivid memories of a mass of blow flies swarming up to greet me as I walked in to sit on the toilet.

In Alexandra, in the winter, the mornings were so cold, we often woke up to hoar frosts with frozen icicles hanging from the trees outside of the train carriage. The summers brought extreme heat and one summer we were placed near a creek where Dad took me swimming with the cockabullies.

Repairs needed were often a long walk up the railway line and would take us away from the carriage for the whole day. Dad would pack us a lunch and make me wear a sunhat as we trekked up the line to the area needing work. While Dad worked on the line, I played in the long grass looking for butterflies, mice, and lizards. The grass went so high, and I was so young that Dad often couldn't see me, and he would keep calling out to ensure that I was there. Lunch was sandwiches and fresh fruit, which we always had in abundance from locals in the area that ran orchards and would give to Dad by the bucketful.

We found a magpie on the rail track that had an injured wing. We named it Maggie and took it home to 703 Highgate and Dad started clipping its wing once the feathers grew back so that it couldn't fly out of the yard. It used to watch Dad plant the vegetable seeds, and then wait till he left and go in with his beak and eat them. It was really tame—if we put our arm down it would climb up and give us kisses. The neighbours next door, used to keep complaining about the noise she made. Once we went to the crib (holiday house/bach) and when we came back, Maggie was gone. We assumed the neighbours took her somewhere. I missed her; she was so much fun.

(Me with Maggie, and Frosty the cat)

(Dad with Frosty)

Jobs often lasted for months at a time, but I normally only stayed in the cabs with him for a few weeks before Dad would take me to stay with one of my siblings or other family members until mum returned home. Sometimes this would take several months.

Normally when mum was home, Dad was away working on the rails. In the early years he came home every weekend, and most of those we would spend up at our separate crib in Wainakarua.

Our crib at Wainakarua was made from an outdated rail carriage that Dad had purchased from work and modified himself. We already owned a section at Wainakarua and Dad paid to have the rail carriage transported there. Once it was in place, he pulled out all of the seats, re-lined and re-wallpapered the inside walls before laying carpet. He installed two sets of bunks, a coal range at the back and a fold up dining table near the door, creating a place where Mum, Dad and I would spend our weekends. If my older siblings didn't have a date for Saturday night, they would often accompany us and sleep on a mattress on the floor.

(Me at the crib, beside our green car)

(Mum and Dad and I at the crib)

During the day, my brothers would head out with rifles and catch Rabbits and Ducks and bring home the game to cook for dinner. This upset me, but mum used to tell me this was just natural - rabbit stew was a popular dish in 1950s Dunedin as there was an abundance of rabbits and a lack of food in the post-depression era. While the boys were away, my mum would go and visit Dad's brother Keith's wife, Aunty Lil, who had a crib on an empty section, two houses down. They often used to work on projects together such as sewing and knitting. While she was visiting, Dad and I would be working outside - scything down the long grass, filling in the long drop and digging a new one and working on wood projects such as handmade furniture, wooden toys, and butterflies which he sold for house exteriors.

When I wasn't spending time with Dad, I used to play with Aunty Lil and Uncle Keith's children, Gary, and Gail. I remember walking to the river to paddle on the stones, in the clearest, most sparkling water I have ever seen. One day I found an injured duck which I carried home to the crib. Mum found a big round plastic bowl which she filled with water and put in the front yard.

(Me taking care of the injured duck)

At our crib, there was an overwhelming scent of sawdust from the nearby sawmill. It smelt like pine. When it got dark, the carriage was lit with kerosene lamps, and we would all head inside to eat tea. After tea I would read my Little Golden Books until it was time to go to sleep. Every few weeks Dad would have to scythe down the long grass as the sawmill owners said it was a fire risk, it was a lot of hard work for Dad, and I remember him sweating profusely.

Financially, things were stable while Dad was alive. Dad made good money working on the railways and up until I was born Mum had been picking up jobs as well. While we weren't rich, Mum never had to worry about money. There was enough to pay the bills, the rent, and groceries. I was sent to a private school and enjoyed weekends away at the crib every weekend. We used to stop in Palmerston and get lunch on the way, ham and mustard sandwiches, and cakes. We used to go shopping regularly, and I would often be bought things - toys and books mainly. I always had nice clothes and was spoiled as the only child now living at home. When Dad died, not only would I miss these luxuries, but Mum would struggle to buy enough food.

During the years that Dad was working in different rail locations, his relationship with Mum deteriorated. As the years went on, and Mum's mental health deteriorated, this took a toll on their marriage. Mum started to imagine things that didn't happen and became an unreliable source of information. Naturally, this created tension in the home.

As things got worse, Dad increasingly volunteered for work that took him away from home and began spending the weekend at the crib by himself. Dad began sending his pay packets back in the mail so that he didn't have to come home on the weekends, and when he did come home, he and Mum would spend almost the entire weekend arguing. Dad had been violent with Mum on and off during the years, but things got worse during this tough time in their marriage. The episode that stuck with me most prominently was one night when Mum was sitting at her table sewing. Earlier that day, a pair of satin kimono pyjamas and a doll had arrived in the mail for me. Dad had ordered the items in the post from a mailer order catalogue with a range of products from Hong Kong. That night I put the new pyjamas on and was looking for my comic book to read in bed. Dad had gone to bed early, as he had to be out of the house early. I found my comic tucked into a stack of newspapers in the living room, so I bent down in the corner of the room to fish it out. Dad came out into the lounge, not realising I was in the room, and started arguing with Mum again. When things escalated, Dad shoved Mum clean off her stool. When Dad stood up, he had blood running down the side of his face, the result of Mum's engagement ring making contact with his face as she went down. Mum took off out the back door and signalled for me to come out with her. Dad, now seeing that I was there, assured me that it was safe to stay, but unsure of what he was capable of, I ran out the door to meet Mum. Mum and I went next door to Mrs. Moody's house and waited until we thought Dad was asleep. We snuck back into the house, through the back door, and Mum climbed into the bottom bunk in my room, leaning a chair against the door so that Dad couldn't come in. When we got up, Dad had gone to work.

    Dad often hid bottles of whiskey in the shed, and I think he had been drinking on this occasion. Mum moved into my room whenever Dad was at home. Dad told my brothers in later years that Mum was "frigid", and Mum told me that she had always hated sex. With that knowledge, I think now the argument was about Mum's reluctance to have sex with him.

    Months after Dad died, I overheard Mum telling my Aunty Phyllis on the phone that if he hadn't passed away, they would have ended up divorced anyway.

The Accident

While my dad was alive, I had grown accustomed to spending a lot of time alone with him, and with both Mum and Dad, in a more managed environment. Since Dad looked out for Mum's mental health, there was no abuse, and her mental illness hadn't impacted on my life.

One weekend in early 1964, everything for me would change.

Dad was sent on a job in Central Otago. Staying in an old carriage as usual, his job that weekend was to repair some railway sleepers which were left beside the track to be used on the main line. While he was cutting and measuring the sleepers, he tripped on an offcut of wood and fell. As he rolled his ankle, he went over the offcut and tore the main artery in his ankle.

Alone and limping, Dad managed to make his way back to the carriage and rested. Although painful, he didn't realise the seriousness of the injury and assumed it was a minor injury such as a sprained ankle. Little did he know that because he already suffered from arteriosclerosis, the injury was much more serious than he realised.

The job, which was supposed to take a week, was unable to be done because of his now limited mobility. Dad's plan was to wait it out in the carriage, till the end of the week when his workmate was due to arrive and take over the job. Dad was scheduled to go home at the end of that week, so he figured he would just pass the time until the next railway worker arrived who could get some help.

As days went by, Dad started to lose feeling in his foot and ankle. When the worker arrived, he was able to organise for Dad to be taken to Dunedin Hospital. Upon arrival, my mother was called. Dad was treated at the hospital and was admitted for a time. When he was discharged, he relied on a walking stick for balance, but was able to get around for a few months or so in that condition. I remember walking to the post office with him two or three times and he seemed to be coping with the pain.

Unfortunately for Dad, he was not making a recovery at home. The ongoing pain prompted him to seek further medical attention, Sadly, it was too late for his foot to be saved, as gangrene had set in, and it was spreading up his leg. He was quickly admitted to a ward and the doctor's decided what the course of action would be. By this stage, the gangrene had reached his knee and it was ultimately decided that the whole leg would have to come off. After the surgery he would have the top part of his thigh remaining.

The surgery took place in the morning and was successful. In the evening, once it was visiting hours, Mum and I went to visit him, once he was awake. When we arrived, he was awake sitting up, having a cup of tea. He said he was relieved that the surgery was over and pulled back the blankets to show Mum and I his bandaged stump. With tears down his face, he mourned for the loss of his old life. We stayed at the hospital for as long as we could before the matron told us that we had to leave. Mum told Dad that she was taking me the next day to buy shoes, and Dad gave her some money out of his hospital locker draw. We went home. That was the last time I saw Dad. I was seven years old. To this day, when I hear songs like *My Dad* by Paul Peterson or *Dance with My Father* by Luther Vandross, I cry.

The next day was my sister June's birthday. Early in the morning, the phone rang. It was the matron delivering the news that Dad had passed away during the night. The cause of death was a blood clot which had developed after the surgery. The clot had travelled up his leg into his lung. If the same surgery was conducted today, Dad would have been given blood thinners before and after surgery in order to avoid developing any clots, so in a way, Dad was a product of his time. Mum didn't say anything to me that morning. Mum spent the rest of the day on the phone, telling relatives what had happened, using a code so that I wouldn't understand.

The next day, Mum told me we were going to stay with her sister, my Aunty Daisy while Dad was in hospital. I didn't understand why we would do this, as we had never stayed with her before.

One night at Aunty Daisy's, I was lying in bed, supposed to be asleep. I could hear voices in the kitchen and snuck out of bed to eavesdrop. Mum and Aunty Daisy were sitting at the kitchen table discussing what was going to happen the next day. The first thing I could make out was Aunty Daisy talking.

> "You will have to tell her, Hazel! The funeral is tomorrow!"

I quietly snuck back into my bed to reflect on what I had just heard, though I had known intuitively that what she said was true. We hadn't visited Dad for days - a strange thing since he had just undergone such a major life-changing operation.

The next morning, I was lying in bed awake when Aunty Daisy called me into the kitchen. Mum was nowhere to be seen. I walked into the kitchen and sat down at the kitchen table. Aunty Daisy told me that the angels had taken Dad to heaven. I sat at the table and cried but was told that I had to get ready to go out. We were due to go to the funeral home that morning to view Dad before his casket was sealed for the funeral. Mum came into the kitchen as Aunty Daisy, and I sat crying and cuddling. She was dressed and ready to go. I went and got dressed and Aunty Daisy and Uncle Herbert dropped us down to the funeral home in South Dunedin.

We went into the front office of the funeral home and were shown through the funeral home by a middle-aged female undertaker who was chubby with glasses. As we started walking toward the viewing room, I started screaming that I didn't want to go. Mum insisted that I go and pulled me by the arm. Luckily the lady that was working there intervened and told my mother that I shouldn't be made to go if I didn't want to. My mother went ahead to view the body and the lady waited with me in the waiting room.

The funeral took place that afternoon. Most of the events of this day are still a blur, but a few key moments still linger in my memory. My mother never cried, not one tear. She displayed no emotion and made sure the day was about her, lapping up the attention. I spent most of the funeral sobbing, with little comfort or even response, from Mum. At the end of the service, when everyone had gathered outside, my older brother Alec leaned down to speak to me.

"It's okay. You've still got me."

This formed the relationship we had throughout my life. My oldest brother couldn't attend the service as he was in prison for burglary. As an adult, Alec and I became close and often talked about Dad.

After the service, the guests all followed us out to the Andersons Bay cemetery where my father was buried in a double plot with a space for my mother above him. I remember clutching onto Alec's leg at the graveside, as we watched my father lowered into the ground.

Afterwards there was a cup of tea put on at Aunty Daisy's home.

After the funeral, we continued to live with Aunty Daisy and Uncle Herbert. We kept getting asked to go home. Mum didn't want to face living in the house by herself, I guess maybe there were too many bad memories, as well as the financial strain.

I didn't realise at such a young age that losing my father would impact me in the ways that it did. Of course, every loss is difficult, but life with Mum, and without Dad, turned out to be vastly different from the life I had known before.

(Last photo taken of Dad, having morning tea with his workmates at the Dunedin railway station. It was in The Evening star newspaper.)

Life After Dad

We ended up staying at Aunty Daisy's house for three months. One morning I was coming up the hallway when I heard Daisy's husband Herbert telling Aunty Daisy that she had to ask Mum to leave, as she had overstayed her welcome. I snuck back to my bedroom where Mum was still asleep. Mum hadn't worked since she had me, so with Dad gone, Mum was worried about how we would manage financially. Staying at Aunty Daisy's meant that her only outgoings were rent for the house we still had at 703 Highgate, Maori Hill. A few days after I overheard Uncle Herbert talking to Aunty Daisy in the kitchen, they drove us home in their car.

Following the death of my Father, I started having really bad nightmares. I used to wake up screaming, and I thought that black crows were swooping in on me. There were great big black wolves, chomping at my face. I also used to have nightmares that the furniture was getting bigger and engulfing me. Normally, when a child is having a nightmare, the parent would come in and cuddle them, to provide some comfort. When Mum heard me having a nightmare, she would come in, drop a cold cloth on my forehead, and walk out, without saying a word. Mum never showed me any affection. I don't ever remember being cuddled or kissed. Not once. But I remember Dad picking me up all the time and cuddling me. In these moments, I wished he was still there to comfort me.

I was plagued by these nightmares, two or three times a week for months. One night, I woke from a nightmare, and was experiencing the usual distress that occurred after one of these nightmares. While I was trying to calm myself down, a glowing light appeared at the end of the bed. I was seven years old, and it's the only time in my life I have ever had a vision like this. The light increased, lighting up the whole room, and in this glowing light, I could see the outline of what looked like Jesus. There was an overwhelming feeling of peace in my room. I immediately calmed down, and the light faded away. I lay there for a long time, trying to process what I had just seen. I never had another nightmare like that, after that night.

Not long after we returned home, my brothers wanted Mum to move to the crib at Waianakarua, but Mum couldn't drive, so its remote location did not really make it a viable option. She decided that since she couldn't live in it, she would sell it. It was still full of our personal possessions, and since my brothers refused to give us a ride up there, it was sold with our belongings in it for very little money. Reflecting back now, this move would have been even further detrimental to my life. Mum would have had a much easier time isolating me, as I would have even had to be home-schooled due to its remote location. I would have no other contact with the outside world.

The house next door from us —705 Highgate—had been vacated while we were away and had been freshly repainted. One afternoon the landlord was touching up the paint outside so Mum went outside to talk to him. I stayed inside and watched out the window. When Mum came back in, she told me that we would be moving into the house next door because the rent was cheaper.

Having decided that moving to this house was the best idea, Mum called up my brothers to find someone to help us shift, but they all said they couldn't help as they were too busy. A couple of weeks later, my mother and I had to move into the house by ourselves. Luckily we were only moving next door since we moved all of our belongings using our green garden wheelbarrow. The boxes of small items we carried across, but the large items were taken by the wheelbarrow. Mum and I had to lift the large wardrobe in my bedroom onto the wheelbarrow and hold it at each end as we wheeled down the street and into the new house.

The house at 705 Highgate was the same size as our current house. The neighbourhood children used to walk past and comment on how it looked like a doll's house with its white paint, and lemon windowsills. After we settled in, Mum placed two concrete planters that she had painted white at either side of the front door and planted them with miniature conifers. The house had two bedrooms. When you entered and turned to the right, you were in the lounge which Mum painted in beige. The floor was covered with an orange bisonia carpet square which she put on her account at Calder MacKay along with some orange cushions to go on our green couch. Calder Mackay was a small department store on Rattray St which let you pay items off. This kind of hire purchase arrangement worked well for Mum, as they would write the items, she took on her card at the store, and then she would come in every Friday and make payments of one pound sterling.

At the lounge window, Mum had cream lace curtains and beige Roman blinds. There was a bay window that was wrapped around the lounge, where Mum kept her Hyde Park pram. This was used for walking our foster babies around Highgate. By this time, we had hired a black and white T.V. set on legs. The brand was 'Gloria'. Mum and I had nothing to do in the evenings, just a radio so we got a tele to watch. We loved all the programmes. Among our favourites were:

- *Peyton Place*
- *Coronation Street*
- *The Avengers*
- *Dr Kildare*
- *The Nurses*
- *Dr Finlay's Casebook*

- *Lancer*
- *Rawhide*
- *The Big Valley*
- *The Untouchables*
- *The Alfred Hitchcock Hour*
- *Petticoat Junction*
- *Bewitched*
- *I Dream of Jeannie*
- *The Andy Griffith show*
- *The Dick Van Dyke show*
- *The Beverly Hillbillies*
- *My favourite Martian*
- *My Three Sons*
- *The Munsters*
- *Green Acres* (which propelled my passion for Yorkshire Terriers)
- And my very favourite, *The Partridge Family*.

As well as these more adult programmes, I loved all the children's programmes, especially *Lassie, Mr Ed* and *Lost in Space*. Since I could sing, I also enjoyed the music programmes, like *C'mon* and *Happen Inn*.

I learnt my 'celebrity idol worship' from my mother. She was always a big fan of the movie stars and singers and was an early version of what is now known as 'fangirls'—a fan, usually a woman, who is obsessed with one or more books, television shows, musical acts, sometimes referred to as 'fandoms'. This vernacular wasn't around back then, but Mum was a textbook fangirl. Mum's favourite musicians were Jim Reeves, and Johnny Cash. She also loved The Seekers and could sing all their songs. She read about her favourite stars in the movie magazines and could tell you all about their lives.

I picked up on this early and took on these same characteristics. Mum's love of these things instilled similar behavioural patterns in myself, although it was directed at different things (as opposed to Jim Reeves, or The Seekers). I'm the same still to this day. I'm known amongst my friends and family as a movie buff and have a wealth of knowledge about various celebrities. As a teenager I developed a massive crush on David Cassidy from *The Partridge Family* and had posters all over the walls in my room which I used to get from the *Tiger Beat* and *16* magazines. When I was buying the magazines from the store one day, the owner tried to offer me some wisdom.

"One day you'll have a boy of your own and you'll forget about these ones."

Many 'boys' later, and I never have forgotten. To this day I am a lifelong fan. I never forgot how David made me feel smiling down at me from the posters. In a way, he kept me going when things were bad. I run a David Cassidy fan group on Facebook now but sadly he passed away a few years ago. What a beautiful and multi-talented man he was.

I also had a huge crush on Craig Scott. Craig was a well-known Kiwi singer who lived in my hometown of Dunedin. He used to appear on television shows like *Happen Inn*. I also liked:

- Bobby Sherman from the 1968 television show *Here Come the Brides*
- James Stacey from the 1968 television show *Lancer*
- Bruce Boxleitner from the 1976 television show *How the West Was Won*
- Rick Ely from the 1970 television show *The Young Rebels*
- Robin Nedwell from the 1969 television show *Doctor in the House*
- Mark Pedrotti from the New Zealand music shows on television

Mum's room at the Highgate house had the same curtaining and blinds as the lounge, with a teal blue candlewick bedspread. Above her bed was a ballet print of a scene from Swan Lake, which I still have. The flooring throughout the entire house was beige linoleum which Mum had installed. Since she couldn't afford the outlay, she paid it off through Calder MacKay, a department store in Rattray St. Mum's bedroom was in the front of the house, facing the road. On the right was the lounge, with my room in behind.

My room was off the living area on the right. I had a set of bunks and a child's bed to accommodate foster children. I slept on the bottom bunk and had two matching orange candlewick bedspreads on the bunk beds. The smaller bed had a heavyweight cotton bedspread made from curtain material that Mum had sewed. The print was kittens playing with pussy willow. My windows were dressed in the same beige Roman blinds, with orange nylon curtaining at each side. Orange was my favourite colour at that time. I had a tallboy with an old gramophone on the top. I used to wind up the handle and play my '78 records on it, as well as on my portable record player for my '45s.

Above my bed was a shelf with six dolls on it, one of which was my Little Tuppence. I had seen many television advertisements of Little Tuppence and had told Mum many times how beautiful I thought she was. One day in Calder McKay, Mum let me buy one doll and one outfit and she added it to her account. I chose the blue bridesmaid outfit and have treasured it ever since. The following year, Mum did the same with a Posing Penny doll, though she couldn't afford to buy an outfit. They fit the same size clothes. Little Tuppence and Posing Penny still reside on a shelf in my lounge.

The dining table sat under the window in the dinette. It was red Formica with steel legs and had four matching red chairs. This room also had a two-seater embossed cream couch where the visitors sat when they came around. The kitchen was a step down and led to the bathroom which consisted of just a bath and a hand basin. Both of those rooms as well as the toilet were painted pale yellow. The separate toilet was where I spent a lot of my time.

She used to lock me in the toilet for the day quite frequently, but on this occasion, I was in there for three days. I remember it getting light and dark three times. I was too scared to break my way out, because of how Mum would react. I would have gotten a hiding. It was freezing cold, wintertime. I remember one night, sitting on the toilet in there, looking at the glistening frost on the floor. Eventually, in the morning she would let me out and put Weet-bix on the table for breakfast. We didn't talk about it. I was just expected to carry on as normal.

Sometimes Mum used other means to lock me up. If I spoke back to Mum, or said anything to her that she didn't like, she would make me get down under my bed, and she would lay my tallboy on its side up against the bed. This would trap me under the bed. I was left there for hours. As a result, I suffer from claustrophobia in my adult life.

The dining room was in behind Mum's room and a step led down into the kitchen. The back door was off the kitchen, and I spent many an afternoon sitting on the back doorstep in the spot where the sun streamed into the kitchen. The backyard had a shed in the middle and a small woodshed.

Across the fence was a set of two flats in a red brick two-storied building. Our house and the flats were separated by an alleyway. The flat underneath was lived in by an elderly couple in their 80s. The top flat was occupied by Pamela, a young mum with a baby. Pamela's husband was abusive, and they were very poor. Her clothes always had holes in them. I liked her a lot, but Mum said that I wasn't allowed to be friends with her because she had gotten pregnant and married at 19, which Mum felt would be a bad influence on me at 15 years old. This was an interesting perspective, given that Mum had become pregnant at the same age, and in the same circumstances.

Sometimes Mum let me bring her washing in for her, from the line at the end of the shared alleyway, but I wasn't allowed to stay. When Pamela moved out, Agnes moved in, she was Samoan and I liked trying the different foods she served. Agnes used to invite us over for tea sometimes, and one night we dined with her guest, a world-famous boxer.

One of my favourite movies as a child was *The Greatest Show on Earth* which used to run sometimes on a Sunday at 2pm. When we moved into the cottage, there were ropes hanging in the woodshed in the backyard that I used to play 'Trapeze', swinging myself from one side of the woodshed to the other. I used to play *The Sound of Music* on the large lawn area behind the shed, twirling around like Julie Andrews. I had a skippy ball, and I would play for long periods, jumping over that. I used to take my battery-operated record player out onto the concrete area outside the back door and listen to music while I danced. One day I was listening to *Let's Get Together* from *The Parent Trap* when Mum called inside for lunch. I left the '45 in the record player with the lid open and when I came back out the record was buckled from the heat of the sun. I was obsessed with Hayley Mills as a child after seeing her in *Pollyanna*. When I got my tonsils out at a private hospital, mum and dad turned up to take me home with the Little Golden Book of *Pollyanna* and a large highland dancer walkie talkie doll. Mum later sold it one time when we didn't have any food.

When I arrived home from school each day, the door was locked, and the key was put in Mum's apron pocket so that I couldn't escape. Sometimes I was allowed to play in the backyard with my dog, and our cats. As I got older, pretend play, fantasy, and acting out movies would become a form of escapism from my abusive life.

Mum's Escalating Struggle with Mental Illness

In the earlier years, mum's mental health was more stable, and Dad's relationship with her was a grounding influence which helped with her depression and anxiety, so she was able to lead as normal a life as possible. Despite what was then diagnosed as melancholia, she was able to stay home and look after the children and hold down her job for a few hours per week. Though she struggled with her mental health all her life, my father's presence meant that it was monitored more closely, and Mum was given appropriate treatments when needed. Dad would see to it that Mum took the antipsychotic medication she was prescribed, but in later years, she refused to take them and flushed them down the toilet. She did, however, choose to take a lot of Valium (now known in New Zealand as Diazepam). In my father's absence, this part of her life became neglected. In the years she and I lived alone, there was no adult present to recognise the signs that things were going downhill.

Mum's father died when she was just 20, and she lost her mother in 1957, at the age of 73. In conjunction with later losing her husband, I am sure that these cumulative losses contributed to the deterioration of her mental health. Mum's mental health issues played out in various settings. When we went out, she said that people were staring at her when they weren't. When she was home, she heard voices but never told me what they were saying. I used to come home from school and find her crying. Mum's closed brethren upbringing was not very pronounced during the years that Dad was alive. After Dad died, Mum's beliefs about God, and the strict religious convictions that she was raised with, became more obvious, and her religious beliefs began to conflate with her mental illness. Her delusions, mixed with her fundamentalist religious beliefs resulted in the abusive environment in which I was raised.

After Dad died, my siblings stopped coming around. They had primarily visited in the past to see Dad, and in his absence, our phone and doorbell stopped ringing. My sister June had left Dunedin, and my brother Eddie was engaged to be married to his girlfriend, Elaine. I remember the night Elaine called and asked me to be a junior bridesmaid for their wedding. I answered the phone, and she said, "I've got something I want to ask you; would you like to be my bridesmaid?" I quickly said yes, and she asked to speak to Mum. I went into the lounge, and Mum went into the phone in the living room to speak with

Elaine. I remember jumping up and down in the lounge with excitement, while they were discussing the details. On the day, I wore a pale pink dress, which was made from a sparkly fabric, with a lace bodice, and a bow at the front. I had beige shoes and gloves. Mum coloured my white church gloves by boiling them with tea bags, to make them beige, to match my shoes. Elaine wanted my hair in a bun on the top of my head, and my mother had no idea how to achieve that. So, on the morning of the wedding, we went to Aunty Phyllis' house to get ready. From there, we went next door to her neighbour, Mrs Janssen who did my hair up with a donut hair accessory. I had very long hair, so it was quite a challenge to pull it all through. It was a very significant day for me, because after the death of my Father, I wasn't allowed to participate in anything.

(My brother Eddie and Elaine's wedding)

With my father's death, also came a dramatic change of finances. The rent at Maori Hill took a big chunk of Mum's widow pension, and there wasn't much money left for food. Mum was also paying off Dad's debts after he died, as his loans did not die with him. Mum was always careful to pay the rent to ensure that we had a roof over our heads, but this was at the cost of having power and food on the table. Mum had an account going at the local shop, but Mr. Soper had set a limit to how much Mum could run her account up to. Once the account was run up, there was no food, and nowhere to go to help. Mum started stealing from the back of the Four Square.

(Mum used to take the alleyway between the shops which led to the back of the Four Square store)

(The Maori Hill shops when I lived there)

The shopkeeper used to leave his fresh produce out the back of the store, in a dark alley. Mum would head up to the store at around 4am with me in my pyjamas, when all the neighbours were asleep pushing her wheelbarrow. We would fill up the wheelbarrow with vegetables and Mum would buy a box of Bisto gravy from the store. The weeks we went to Four Square, we ate well. The weeks when Mum didn't steal from the alley, we had two slices of bread with gravy on it for dinner, or cabbage soup. During those weeks I also didn't take any lunch to school. Mum never went for these nightly visits when she had money on her shop account to use, or spare money that week. It was something she did out of necessity. When our neighbours went on holiday with their teenage daughter Lynette to their bach, at Taieri Mouth,

Mum used to go and take something out of their freezer which sat in an unlocked shed in the backyard. Mum never took more than she needed - a bag of peas, or a tray of chops. She always stole on an as-needed basis. She often talked about the guilt of it and wondered if God would be upset with her.

    Mum's pension used to come in the mail as a cheque, and Mum would have to walk up to the post office each week to cash it. When she felt that she had something to sell, she used to invite dealers up to sell things. I would often see her going through her jewellery and picking out something that could make some money to buy food or she sold her mum's china. I remember all the beautiful carnival glass we had to sell.

    On a Sunday morning, we would get up early, get dressed up with a hat and gloves, and walk to the Kaikorai Gospel Chapel on Taieri road. Sometimes we used to go to my Aunty Phyllis' home after the service and stay for dinner. She lived at 86 Walton St, Kaikorai Valley, which was within walking distance from our church. I always liked when we didn't go straight home, because Mum would say that Sunday was God's Day, and we weren't allowed to watch television, or have the radio on. The choices for how to spend the day would be to pray or read the Bible.

    Aunty Phyllis' cooking was delicious, and she always had about half a dozen tins full of baking. Mum was always known for outstaying her welcome, and I would fall asleep on the sofa in front of the T.V. She would wake me up at midnight to walk home along Highgate from Phyllis' home on Walton St to our home at Maori Hill. I'd always start asking to go home about 9pm because I was tired, but she was too busy talking. My Aunty would always agree with me. We frequently had foster babies in the pram, walking at that hour of the night as well. One night we were approached by the Police to see if we were okay. My Aunty used to play the piano for us and give us apples to take home from her fruit trees. I used to stay with her sometimes when Mum went to the mental home. I always wanted to stay with her because she had a flash house with carpet, and we ate good food. All their children had grown and left home. She lived there with my Uncle Roy and two caged birds. I was allowed to play the piano and she had one wall in her lounge covered in mirror tiles. I used to practice my ballet in front of it, that I had been taught at Columba College. Her house was pretty much in the same street as Balmacewen Intermediate, which meant I could still attend school while I stayed there.

(Aunty Phyllis, Uncle Roy, and Granddaughter)

The years went by, one after another, and Mum and I became more isolated from other people. The only visitors were my brothers occasionally, but they were busy with their own families, working to try and survive. My oldest brother Brian was in and out of jail for petty theft, and at one stage his wife, Mary, and three children came to live with us while he was inside. I loved it because it gave me someone to play with, and the abuse stopped. But Mum and Mary had a falling out, and she abruptly took the children to Christchurch.

(Mum and I with Brian's oldest child Bryan)

(Me with Jo-ann beside me and Judy on the far right, Brian's daughters)

    Whenever my brothers came to visit, they used to throw me up towards the ceiling and say, "Who's girl are you?" My answer was always Alec. For some reason, he was always my favourite, even though my brother Brian had my name tattooed on his arm, which he got done when I was born. Mum was in the maternity home, and Brian went and parked outside and tooted for her to look out the window. He stood on the roof of his car, when she came to the window. He made a motion of a baby by rocking his arms, with excitement. He yelled out, and asked what I had been called, and how to spell it, and then went straight to the tattoo parlour to get my name tattooed on.

My brothers used to visit more when Dad was alive. None of them got on too well with Mum. My sister lived in a house in Wright St, Kaikorai, but she moved with her family to Central Otago when her husband John got a farm manager's job.

Occasionally, Mum and I would catch the train to June and John's there and stay for a week or so, or I would stay with her when Mum went back into the mental home. I loved it. She had three sons that were not much younger than me. We used to play out on the paddocks, and feed the chickens, turkeys, and pigs. We rode horses and swam in the creek. We used to play *Lost in Space, The Man From U.N.C.L.E, Thunderbirds,* and "Cowboys and Indians". The time I spent there was wonderful - I got to run around the farm and spend time with my nephews Colin, David, and Simon.

(Me with Kimmy my Pomeranian, on the farm)

Sometimes I would stay with June's husband's parents, Dora, and Joe at their cottage in Cromwell, Central Otago. I remember sitting in front of their warm coal range, in the middle of frosty winters. There were other children in the neighbourhood, and they would all flock outside when they saw the trucks coming, as they would be handed something to eat. Sometimes it was apples from the produce trucks, but I remember being handed a slice of luncheon and cold saveloys from the butchery truck drivers when they came to sell their goods.

One night, while I was staying with my sister June, it was getting dark. Colin, David, Simon, and I were still outside. We had wandered into a paddock that had a bull. John had searched for us for a long time. When he found us, he was furious, and he hit all of us with the jug cord when we got back home.

"Do you know what would have happened if that bull had come out?!?!"

I remember having bruises on my hips the next morning, but for me that was normal. In those days parents felt that they owned their children and could do what they liked with them. John hit his own children as well, so it seemed natural that he would treat me the same as his other children when I would stay there.

When Mum used to call to say she was coming back home, I would cry. Mum's increasingly brethren beliefs were causing the home to be a very restrictive and volatile environment. Being at the farm was a freedom that I never had at home.

After Dad had passed away, a few months later, Mum started taking foster babies again. Each baby paid around $5 a week which helped. This gave us enough money to eat properly, for a few days even though Mum had to buy extra milk. Mum sometimes took more than one baby at a time if they were siblings. This doubled our payment. Having foster babies in the house meant we could eat better. We used to have 'meat and three veg' meals for dinner, and a slice of some sort of cake for pudding, or jelly. Mum used to make baked rice pudding in the oven, with nutmeg sprinkled on top. Semolina, Steamed Pudding, Tapioca, and Bread and Butter pudding with coconut on top were also favourites. During these times I also had chocolate chip sandwiches (butter and chocolate chips sprinkled over) to take to school for lunch.

(Me with one of the foster babies Karen Mataura. I am around age 8)

One of our longest placements was John (and his cousin Paul at one stage). John was with us from the time he was a baby till he went to school. Mum used to keep him in a zip up bag with no sleeves, and he would wake up early and jump into bed with me. When we heard Mum wake up, I used to grab John and run him back to his own bed where he slept at the other side of my room. I remember him, around three years old, jumping out of the bed in a hurry, scrambling to run back to his bed in an infant sleep bag. I still laugh when I envision it. If Mum had caught him in my bed, we would have both got a hiding, because Mum would have made it into something sexual. That was the first place her mind always went.

When Mum was changing the male baby's nappies, she used to say that "he's going to hurt somebody with that penis someday" and stick the nappy safety pin in their penis. Sometimes, Mum would also turn them over and backhand them on the bottom before doing the nappy up. The male foster babies were put into zipper bags and blindfolded during the day. They had to sit on the couch for hours and were not allowed to see her. For Mum, all males would grow up to become sexual deviants who were going to hurt women.

John slept in a sleeveless bag until he was over four years old, but sometimes wore it during the day as well. His arms were trapped inside the bag all day and night, and his movement was restricted. As a result of this lack of stimulation, John was developmentally delayed, and didn't meet his milestones. This was probably not surprising, given that he spent his life in a bag, blindfolded sitting on the couch, and the other half in bed. Mum hated males and overall, the girls were treated better than the boys.

The female foster babies wore frilly dresses and ate in a high chair at the table. Mum kissed them on the head and let me carry the girl babies around on my hip and play with them. There were no blindfolds, or bags. Their experience was very different to that of the boys.

It is well documented now that the foster system in New Zealand is full of historical abuse. Mum was not properly vetted to check for a history of mental illness. Social workers did not come to the house. Once a baby was placed with us, there was no state presence, and Mum was able to care for them as she saw fit.

While we resided in Highgate, Mum befriended a man, Victor, who owned a second-hand shop in Frederick St.

(Victor Nelson's second-hand shop)

Victor soon learned that Mum was a widow and started coming to the door in a taxi with cartons of groceries. This helped us out with food, but he made me uneasy. One day he came to the house and sat at the dining table with me while Mum was in the kitchen making him a cup of tea. He took one of the oranges and placed it down my pants and proceeded to put his hand in to fish it out. I never told Mum about what Victor did but was relieved when she broke things off with him. If I had told her she would have said I instigated it, that was how her mind worked.

I started at Maori Hill school after Dad died, when we returned home from Aunty Daisy's. Mum said she couldn't afford the fees, and why should I go to a private school when my siblings went to state ones. I loved being able to wear dresses and being liberated from wearing a uniform. I attended Maori Hill school until I turned 10.

(I am pictured 5th from the left, front row.)

The principal Mr. Sinclair was very passionate about mathematics and used to slam his ruler down on the desk if I didn't know the answer. This frightened me and led me to increasingly despise maths as a subject at school. To this day, I struggle with numbers, and I believe that the actions of my teacher, which put me off learning, contributed to this.

(Maori Hill School at the time that I went. The building has now been demolished)

Toward the end of my time at Maori Hill, I had a teacher—Mr Heperi—who taught us short poi, te rakau sticks, and waiata for our end of year concert. At the time, Mum and I had my sister-in-law Mary Paki Constable and her children living with us, and I found the Maori culture resonated with me. Mary lent me an authentic Maori costume to wear for the concert. I felt so special in my authentic indigenous outfit, knowing it was full of family history, since most of the children just had homemade ones, a black cotton skirt that their mum had run up on the machine. I still remember all of the Maori lyrics to the three songs I learned for this.

I still recall the years I spent at Maori Hill school fondly, I had friends that were kind to me including a girl named Janis Aldcroft who lived a few doors down from me. I was allowed to go to her birthday parties because Mum knew her mother. A few weeks after I started at Maori Hill school, I had forgotten my lunch and mum turned up at morning tea time to bring it to me, I was standing in the playground holding hands with my friend Janis, mum walked over, slapped my hand down and then smacked me across the face in front of the other pupils. I didn't know at the time what I had done wrong but in later years looking back it was about her homophobia. I often think now, she would be turning in her grave about our acceptance of same sex couples, and the legalisation of same sex marriage in New Zealand.

When I was staying with my Aunty Phyllis, a school friend Madelon was having a birthday party, she lived in a house in front of my Aunty and her and Madelons mum used to chat over the fence, so I was invited, she was turning nine, I wore a lemon nylon ruffle dress and I tied a yellow satin ribbon in my hair, 'Alice in Wonderland' style. When I was a child there were stretch coloured hair bands called 'Alice bands' of which I had quite a few.

I remember admiring the lovely black and white chequered lino when I walked into their home, it was very flash compared to my humble upbringing. Madelon got the Mary

Poppins LP record and the "Sindy as Mary Poppins" doll. I was extremely envious. I bought both on Trade Me a few years ago.

In those earlier years after Dad had passed, I enjoyed the time that I spent at school, and with friends. Whilst my time at home was troubling, I still managed to get some time away. In addition, because I was young, Mum didn't have to exert too much control over me. This changed as I got older.

Balmacewen Intermediate Years

During those first four years of my Father's absence, I had to try and come to terms with the grief, while my mother would not allow it. I wasn't allowed to grieve because Mum wasn't. While I was trying to figure out who I was now, Mum was tightening the reins. Life without Dad was starting to take shape and was taking a turn for the worst.

I was eleven when I started at Balmacewen Intermediate, in 1968. Mum couldn't afford my uniform, so she applied for assistance from an association which provided funding for the children of ex-servicemen who were now deceased. She went and filled out a form detailing what the money would be used for and was granted the cost of a brand-new uniform. In later years, they also paid for my braces. The grant didn't cover enough to buy shoes so on my first day I went wearing an out of place pair of Charlie Browns. To make them last longer, Mum had attached metal plates to the heel and the toe, making me sound like a tap dancer every time I walked. Naturally, the kids didn't have to look very hard to find a reason to start bullying me. I wasn't used to bullying as I had never encountered it before. Unfortunately, this wasn't the only thing they bullied me about. I had very long hair and they called me a witch. My time at Balmac was a living hell. I got beaten up during the day, by my peers, and then came home and was subjected to the same by my mother. When I told Mum she said I deserved it.

After Dad died, I stopped speaking. Mum took me to the GP who referred me to a psychologist. By the time I got to intermediate, I had been diagnosed with 'emotional disturbance', which is now known as Post Traumatic Stress Disorder. I didn't speak at school and was constantly falling behind in my schoolwork. My reports always remarked that I had difficulty concentrating and really showed signs of being emotionally disturbed.

The main bully was an eleven-year-old boy named Leslie. Though I never spoke to him, he used to wait until the teacher wasn't looking to punch my arms. His best opportunities happened when we were lining up for sport, or in the playground, I was constantly black and blue with bruises he caused me. When I tried to talk to Mum about it, she demanded to know what I had done to provoke his behaviour and that I probably deserved it.

The toilets were also out of bounds for me, as two girls, Christine, and Gaynor, guarded the place during morning tea and lunch breaks. If I tried to enter, they would call me names like

'Maggot' and 'Cunstable' and beat me, or trip me as I came in. Because I couldn't go to the bathroom and I had such a long walk home, I used to wet my pants before I reached the house. When my mother saw me, I got a hiding for having an accident at my age. The bullies also used to say "Ha ha! Cunstable's father's dead, and her brother is a jailbird". They also told me how ugly I was and that they were sorry that I was born. In class, I couldn't put my hand up because they would slap it down and they shoved me out of line and took my space when we were doing activities at school.

When I was waiting to audition for the school choir they came past, howling with laughter because they were sure that I couldn't sing. Most of my family could sing, a gift I have passed on to my children. The music teacher Judy Farris proved them wrong and put me in the special choir, of which there were only ten of us. We were picked from the usual 'normal' choir which we used to lead. I have always been able to sing in tune -a gift that I inherited from Mum. In Mum's earlier life, she did backup singing for The Tumbleweeds on a couple of their vinyl records. The Tumbleweeds were a famous Dunedin band and were hugely influential on country music in New Zealand. They were the first country band in New Zealand to be recorded. Their early 1949 single 'Maple on the Hill' became a standard song for country music performers in New Zealand and went on to sell 80,000 copies. Mum was good friends with Nola Hewitt who performed vocals, double bass, ukulele, guitar, and mandolin for the group. I'm not sure how Mum came to perform on the track for The Tumbleweeds, but I followed in her tradition—I went on to sing in a band, perform in many choirs, enter talent quests, taught singing and sang and danced in musical theatre, which in my later years, I directed.

There were a few classmates who used to stick up for me. Most of the kids there set out to make my time a nightmare. The teaching staff were no better, except for Miss Sue Hannon, who I looked up to.

Mum used to frequently sleep in and not get me to school until assembly had already started. I was often dragged to the back of the hall and grilled for this, in front of all my classmates. Mum had a habit of doing the housework in the middle of the night and going to bed around 5am. She frequently was sweeping under my bed or coming in and out putting clothes away in my drawers and I couldn't get any sleep, hence why she slept in in the mornings and so did I. When my classmates had to pick teams for class activities, I was always left standing at the end and had to be assigned a team. Nobody wanted to choose the little girl who never spoke. Every part of my intermediate experience was stifled, and each day was filled with dread. Every morning Mum would give me Weet-bix, and I would vomit them up on the way to school, because I was so nervous about what the day would bring. While I had been used to being beaten at home, at least I had been given a few hours during the day as respite. At intermediate, I was subjected to abuse from the time I got to school, till the time I went to bed.

After a while, I decided that it's better to deal with the devil you know and started faking illness to try and avoid going to school. At least if I stayed home, I would only get beaten by one person, not multiple. I used to put my toothbrush down my throat and vomit into the basin, then call mum and show her.

A few of the boys in my class made my time there more bearable. Linden Davey, Peter Brogan, Kerry Swete, who I was told sadly died during a boating accident. Also, Janet Horn, who used to get me to go to her house to feed her pet lamb when she had something on after school. I loved feeding the wee lamb. I have never forgotten these people.

For most of my life I was kept home from school because I had physical bruises, another reason the kids used to tease me, said that I was wagging, and I found it hard to keep up with my school work and all my school reports reflect this. They say Debra's frequent absences are causing her to fall behind.

Life With Mum

While we were living at Maori Hill, a couple of times we got the train up to Christchurch during the school holidays and we stayed with a friend of Mum's called Avis, who she met in the mental home. Avis had a nervous breakdown and ended up in care at the same time as Mum. She lived with her husband, and her son who went to a local university, he lived nearby on campus. While we were staying there, Avis' husband used to take us for drives, and take us places, like through the Lyttelton tunnel, or out to Rangiora for lunch, where my uncle George's ex-wife owned a hotel.

(Me at the Rangiora hotel with the owner's dog)

One night, Avis' son came home for tea. I had been watching *C'mon* and Ray Columbus had been on with his single "She's a Mod". I was setting the table for tea, and in walks Avis' son, with his friend Ray Columbus. I stood there staring, but Avis was oblivious to who he was. I was nine years old, and still remember it vividly. Mum smiled knowingly at me, and we all sat down to eat. I was so starstruck that I struggled to eat anything.

(Me at Avis's house)

(Mum and I and my friend from down the road, Janis who we bumped into. She used to go to the *Mardi Gras* alone, which my mother wasn't happy about.)

Dunedin used to hold a *Mardi Gras* once a year, in the Octagon. The following year, after we had been staying at Avis' house,

Ray Columbus was singing on the back of a truck for the *Mardi Gras*. Mum and I waited at the side of the truck for him to finish performing, and when he came down, he stood and chatted with us for a while, having remembered us from the dinner. We also attended the Winter Show each year, which was held in the building that Brown's Furniture Dealers in Crawford St was in. The shop was vacated every year for the event, and stalls, rides and other carnival attractions filled the space. Mum would save up all year, in a jar, for us to go. We only had enough money for the admission price, and something to eat, and a doll. In my younger years, Mum and I would choose a hot dog on a stick to eat. When I was older, and became vegetarian, I then swapped the hot dog for the candy floss. The highlight of the Winter show was getting to choose a doll on a stick. They had hundreds of Kewpie dolls lined up to choose from, in beautiful dresses, covered in glitter and lace. I gazed up at all the bright colours and couldn't decide which one to choose. There were several rows of dolls, all with various prices, but I had to choose from the bottom row—the most inexpensive ones. Since we didn't celebrate Christmas or birthdays in my house, it felt like a big decision, since it was the only gift I would receive all year. After a while, when the dresses started getting dusty and faded, Mum would throw the whole thing—doll and outfit—into the fire drum and dispose of it.

(Mum and I at the *Mardi Gras*)

Mum met a few ladies in the mental homes that she kept in touch with. One was named Mary Buchanan. She lived on the main road in Ravensbourne and had undergone so much electroconvulsive therapy (shock treatment) that she didn't function normally anymore. I used to dread her visits to our house. She would stand in the doorway talking to Mum and then start smashing her head on the door frame. She would stop suddenly, and then go on talking to Mum as if nothing had happened. She lived with her husband Lou, who Mum suspected was abusive as Mary had told her so. Sometimes we would go to her house to visit. Her teenagers—Pamela and Kenny—would crack eggs on her head as they walked past and spit on her. I would spend time with her son Murray who was my age while Mary and Mum were talking. Mum was so disgusted about Mary's teenager's behaviour toward their mother, that we stopped going to her house.

Mum had also befriended a nice lady called June Carter, who had a lot of children that she used to bring with her. Marilyn, Beverly, Pauline, Dianne, and Keith were around my age, and I used to have a great time with them. When June brought the kids over, we would play records or play with my dolls.

When Dad was alive, I got Christmas and Birthday presents. After Dad, Christmas was just another day. Mum never bought me any presents and anything that was given to me was confiscated and re-gifted to others. Aunty Daisy used to drop off gifts for me at Christmas. One year she dropped off a French perfume and left it at the front door. I heard the door first and saw Aunty Daisy out the window, returning to her car. I hurried out to the door to unwrap it before Mum realised what was going on and she snatched it out of my hand. It was wrapped and gifted to someone else for Christmas. Another year, my brother Alec's wife Lorraine brought me a baby pink lace full petticoat with a pair of matching pants. It was wrapped in tissue paper in a flat box and was so beautiful. Mum waited for Lorraine to leave and wrapped it up for someone else. Mum didn't make Christmas dinner. We didn't celebrate anything, including Jesus' birth. My birthday was the same, except for one year. On my 12th birthday, I came home after school and there was a birthday card on the table, with a bag of cherries. She had never bought me a gift before, despite my efforts to do something for her birthday every year. She used to like Milko bars, so I used to go to the shop on her birthday on the way home, buy one and wrap it in a page from my school book. They used to sell these little gift cards that looked like the Christmas ones without the adhesive on the back. They were two cents each, so I would choose one with a cat on and write a little birthday message on it and put it with the gift. The first time I celebrated Christmas I was living with my brother after I had run away from home, and he bought me a gift, along with the gifts he gave his children.

In later years when I was in my 20s, she would send me flowers for my birthday. A 'posy bowl'- a small green plastic bowl with flowers pushed into wire. I wondered why she would do this for me when I had my own family and not when I needed to her recognise my birthday when I was a child. I've always enjoyed giving people little gifts and would rather give than to receive. I like making people happy.

Mum did have kindness, but it was directed at strangers, not me. One memory I have of this is when we were at the Dunedin North Intermediate fair, one Saturday. My Mum noticed a girl with a baby, aged around six months old. The baby was in a pram which was in very poor condition. It was dirty, ripped, and broken. Mum approached the girl and asked her name. Her name was Cath. Mum told Cath that she had a nicer pram in her basement at home, which she could give to her. Mum asked for her address and said that she would drop the pram down to Cath's home, later in the week. Cath was living near the Dunedin Botanical Gardens, so we walked the Pram down to the North end, with no baby in it, to her house. Cath invited us in for a cup of tea. While we were drinking our tea, Cath's husband came home, and she made him 'bubble n squeak' in a fry pan with a couple of sausages. Cath didn't appear to eat anything herself, which, in conjunction with the condition of her original baby pram, I assume was due to their financial situation.

    Another example of her kindness towards others, is when Mum had knitted a gorgeous teal Angora cardigan and had only worn it once. Mum was fostering a baby at the time who had been placed with us for about three months. She was a little Maori girl, who had arrived with no clothing or possessions of her own. Mum had bought her all of the items she would need, including beautiful frilly dresses, and the little over pants with frills on the bottom. Her Mother had been in prison for shoplifting. Upon her release, she came straight to our house in a taxi to pick up her baby. The taxi waited while she picked up the baby, as they were both heading to the airport, to return home to her family in the North Island. When she arrived, she was wearing a cotton sleeveless dress, despite it being wintertime.

When Mum answered the door, she noticed how underdressed she was for the time of year, and put her hands on the cold arms of the baby's mother. She commented that her skin was freezing and invited her inside. Mum went to her bedroom drawer and took out the teal cardigan she had knitted for herself. She took it out to the lounge and put it on the baby's Mum. She was very grateful and commented on how beautiful it was. After she left I said, "Mum you loved that cardi!" and she said "oh, I can knit another one". But she never did.

Reflecting on it, I wonder if Mum did these kind things for the attention that she garnered from them. It's difficult for me to accept that she was kind to others because of her Christian beliefs, or because she had a generous heart when my experience with her had been so radically different.

Mum used to burn our household rubbish in a drum in the backyard. One Saturday afternoon when I was 11, she had left the shed door ajar, and I went in to look around. I found some white slingback shoes that were miles too big and put them on. I walked up and down the concrete path in them and then took them off to put them back in the shed. When I turned around, I noticed three beautiful dresses hanging on the back of the door. One was a full-length ballerina dress in white and there were two debutante dresses. One had a pink satin bodice and a tulle skirt, and the other one was lemon chiffon with rosettes all over it. Mum was busy at the rubbish drum, so I went over and said,

"Mum, can I try on those beautiful dresses in the shed? I want to play 'grown-ups'."

Without speaking she pushed me down on the grass, grabbed the dresses from the back of the door and threw them in the burning drum. Then she glared at me.

"See how grown up you'll look now!"

I ran inside and cried because I blamed myself for the destruction of those beautiful dresses, if I hadn't said anything they would not have been destroyed.

During our years at our house in Maori Hill, I used to breed baby mice, which I sold to the pet shops. When the mice became old or sick, mum used to flush them down the toilet which made me cry. I also had a cream pet rat named Tara. I had a wee bitser dog named Sally. She was a ginger colour. But when we were moving to our state house, Mum said the section wasn't suitable and we had to rehome her. She went to an older lady in Scarba St, and I used to walk up from Otago Girls and visit her.

We always owned a lot of cats, which I spent hours with. Mum used to breed and show them.

(Me receiving a cup for one of my cats)

NOTED JUDGE OF CATS TO SPEAK IN CITY

Advice has been received by the Otago Cat Fanciers' Club that Miss Elizabeth Yorke, world-renowned judge of cats, has left England to judge at the Auckland Show. The club made arrangements for Miss Yorke to give a public address on cats in Dunedin.

At the annual meeting on Tuesday it was decided to hold the 1956 annual show at the Agricultural Hall on July 21.

Officers elected were:—

Patron, the Mayor, Mr Wright; president, Mr H. L. Boock; vice-presidents, Mr C. Aberdeen and Mrs T. Munro; secretary, Mr A. D. McNamara; treasurer, Mr P. Smith; committee, Mesdames J. Aberdeen, E. Cleaver, H. Constable, E. Mussen, A. Miller, F. McNamara, McLeod, F. Smith, Misses D. Mussen, J. McLeod; Mr A. Constable, Messrs A. Peat, N. Stevens, R. Wallis.

My mother and father were one of the founders of the Otago Cat Fancier's Club, and Dad built all the cages for the inaugural show. When kittens were born at home, if they were not ginger, tortoiseshell, white or cream, Mum would fill up a bucket of warm water and drown them, as they were not saleable. I started hating when I knew the cats were having kittens. I would see her drowning them from the kitchen window and would be standing there with tears running down my face. To this day I have always been a great animal lover and could never do such a thing. I have been involved in animal rescue work for many years and am a life member of SAFE (Save Animals from Exploitation).

Mum was going into hospital for surgery, after finding a lump in her breast which turned out to be benign. We had a few cats at the time, but one of them - my cat Pollyanna - had a litter of kittens who were all riddled with ringworm on the face, like their mother. While Mum used to drown newborn kittens, these ones were more than a month old. Mrs Ritchie, who ran the Blue Cross Animal Welfare Society, had offered to take the healthy cats, but could not take the ones with the ringworm. In normal circumstances, when you go into hospital, you ask a family member, or friend, to come and feed your pets. Unfortunately, Mum's behaviour had driven my brothers away, and so she had nobody to ask. She called Colin Aberdeen, the vet who was part of the Cat club she was in and asked if he would come to the house and euthanise the unhealthy kittens. I was standing watching out the kitchen window when he arrived. He went into the yard, picked up each kitten by the scruff of the neck, injected them with a needle, and dropped them back to the ground where they quickly died. When it came to my cat Pollyanna, he did the same thing, but she ran around the shed, then to the window I was watching out and spun around frantically several times, before dropping dead in front of me. Having witnessed this, I have never wanted to go in and witness any of my pets, when they have been put to sleep. By the time Mum did go in for surgery, I had also lost another treasured pet. Mum and I were in town one day, and we went into the John Dean Garden Store. Mum was looking for plants.

When we went down the back of the shop, there was a litter of four kittens playing amongst the plants. The mother cat was a pedigree Persian, but she had gotten pregnant with a domestic cat, so the owner of the store was giving the kittens away. Mum went up to the counter and asked if he was looking for a home for those kittens? He said,

"By all means, take one".

We went to the back to watch them play. Mum wanted the tortoiseshell patched kitten, but the one I wanted was fluffier, and white with a black patch on its back. We stood there for ages trying to decide, before Mum went back to the man and asked if we could take two. We called a taxi and went home with the two kittens. Mum noted that one of them looked like it had small ginger pebbles on its back, and suggested we call it "Pebbles", after the character from *The Flintstones*. I then suggested we call the other "Bam Bam". A couple of months later, we entered them in the Otago Cat Fancier's Club Show, and they won a lot of prizes. Pebbles was killed on the road, as we lived on a main thoroughfare.

Admittedly, Mum didn't have very good physical health. She suffered from angina and had undergone several operations to try and correct issues with her women's health. She was often laying on the couch when I arrived home from school with bladder pain which I also suffer from now. She had a few minor health scares which turned out to be incidental. She suffered from migraines. Frequently, when I came in from school, she would unlock the back door and go to sleep on the couch. I would tiptoe around, so as not to wake her up. I would go into my room and do homework until she woke up and asked me to make her Maggi soup. Mentally, on top of her schizophrenia and bi-polar disorders, she also suffered from anxiety. I'm sure it was a lot for her to deal with. She also had severe OCD, if she was talking on the phone and noticed a crooked mat or picture, she would put the phone down, go and fix it and go back to the phone, i have inherited this slightly where i like things to be perfect with no mistakes.

My sister June, my cousin Gail, my Aunty Daisy, and my brother Brian used to ask if they could take me out. June and Gail used to take me to Elvis movies. I'm still a fan of his and have all his movies on DVD. Aunty Daisy took me to her friend's farmlet to feed the baby lambs in spring. Brian took me to antique auctions out of town. When they asked Mum, she would take me aside and say, "I might not be alive when you get back." Her attempts to manipulate me did not succeed. It used to upset me, but my family took me anyway. I always had a good time away from her and that mundane existence, and lo and behold, she was still alive when I got back.

Our doctor suggested I go to the Roxburgh Children's Health Camp. This operated from the early 1940s year-round and was regarded as beneficial for children who were unwell—both physically, or mentally. The camp consisted of four main buildings - a dining and common room, two dormitories and an open-air school. It also had a swimming pool, sand pit, playing fields and playground. Roxburgh in central Otago was chosen for its location, so that children throughout Otago and Southland, aged between five and 12 could attend. This is now known as one of New Zealand's oldest social services for children. It aimed to provide children with the benefits of sunshine, rest, fresh air, and regular, healthy meals which included fresh meat and vegetables and a pint of milk. The doctor felt that this would be a good environment for me. There were nurses on sight, and I would be well looked after, but Mum wouldn't allow it. She wouldn't let me out of her sight.

In contrast to my experience at Balmacewen Intermediate, my time at Otago Girls High School was enjoyable, there was no bullying and I had lots of friends as by then I was coming out of my shell, in particular: Anne-Marie Armishaw, Glenda Broadley (who sadly died in a car crash a few years after leaving school), Jan Halberg, Madelon Janssen, Sue Graveson, and Margaret Smitheram (whom I later went to live with her and her family).

When I first started at Otago Girls, I used to come home for lunch. I brought my friend Anne home for lunch one day without asking. Mum opened the door, looked at Anne, slapped me in the face, and dragged me inside. I was made to eat my lunch while Anne waited outside. Mum frequently used to backhand me on the face, and her engagement ring would cut my lip or cheek.

(Me at 14 with my Pomeranian 'Kimmy')

When I turned 15 in December 1972, a friend of mine from my class, Marilyn, came to school and said she had got a job for the school holidays at Woolworths. So, I went home that night and asked Mum, and she said I could get the job if I gave the money to her. The next day I went and applied at lunchtime and got a call that night to say that I had a job too. I worked there for six weeks at the end of the year in the cosmetic department. I loved it and didn't want to go back to school the following year. They had permanent jobs available, but Mum made me go back to school. I worked there again for three weeks at the end of the first term. They were a nice bunch of people, and they took back the same students each school holiday period. I had a crush on a boy that went to St. Paul's, who used to empty the rubbish bins under the counter. He lived in Montague St, North East Valley and his name was Richard Davies. I gave him my number, but when he called, Mum slammed the phone down in his ear. I wasn't allowed to have friends, and I wasn't allowed to talk on the phone. If anyone called for me, Mum would hang up in their ear. According to Mum, it was her phone since she paid for the bill. When I went to live with Aunty Daisy, she said that phones belonged to a house, and that anyone in the house was free to use the phone. Mum's restrictions on the phone were just another way of isolating me from my peers, and from others outside the home.

Mum never talked about sex, or periods. Those things were taboo in our house. I was extremely naive. I remember the day I got my period. I was 15 and was the last in my friend group to get it. It was during the school holidays, and I had blood when I wiped in the toilet. I called Mum in, in a panic. She said that it would come each month and that once this started, the boys would start "sniffing around". I came out of the toilet, and she smacked me across the face. I wasn't sure what I was being slapped for, so I asked.

> "You've been having sex. That's what brought it on early."

I certainly had not had sex; I had never had a boyfriend. When I left home, I thought that you had to be married to be able to get pregnant. That God would give married couples a child after they had been married for a while, which is how I ended up becoming pregnant at such a young age.

Because of the financial strain in our household, the water heater was only turned on each Saturday. That meant 'period' week was very long, and I couldn't clean myself until Sunday, no matter when my period came on. I was able to have a small basin wash each morning, using the recycled water from my hot water bottle, given to me the night before. While this was warmer water than the cold water from the tap, the rubber smell that it had used to make me feel nauseated. This water allowed me to wash my face, hands, and a quick wash anywhere else that was needed. In addition, the only cleaning products allowed in my house were cakes of Sunlight soap. Mum believed that personal hygiene and cleaning products contained too many chemicals, so I had to wash my hair with it, and bathe with it. Mum used it to clean the dishes with the soap in a small wire basket with a handle and used to grate it into the Wringer washing machine. To this day, I can't stand the smell.

When I was 15, Mum's dream of getting a state house came true. We were offered a home at 79 Columba Ave, so we moved. The rent would be much more affordable, and it offered more security as our landlord had been hinting that he was considering selling our house at Highgate.

During the years that we lived at Maori Hill, Mum frequently used to hit me with the 'cat of 9 tails'. It was a barber strap, made from leather and used for sharpening the shaving tools. On the end was a metal part which was used to hang it in the barber shops. Of course, she used the metal end right at my legs. I used to jump on the bed with my legs tucked under me, but she pulled me by the hair down onto the floor and hit me hard. When her temper flared, her eyes would blaze, this really scared me.

When we were packing to move from Maori Hill to the new house in Columba Ave, I took the Cat of nine tails strap and threw it into the empty section, behind our old house, in the long grass. When we moved to the new house, Mum kept looking for it. Of course, I didn't know where it was.

Things got worse after I turned 16. I was now of legal age and should have been allowed some freedom.

Columba Ave

When I got to age 16, I was allowed some small freedoms, if they directly benefited Mum.

Mum signed the lease for the new house in Columba ave when I was 15, but I was 16 by the time we move into it, in 1973. The Department of Social Welfare (now called Work and Income New Zealand or WINZ) paid for a removal truck from a company called 'Didhams'. Didham's was a fleet of delivery trucks owned by J. L. Didham and was the first Dunedin delivery truck service. It was quite common for new families who were offered a state house to be offered a truck to assist them with moving in.

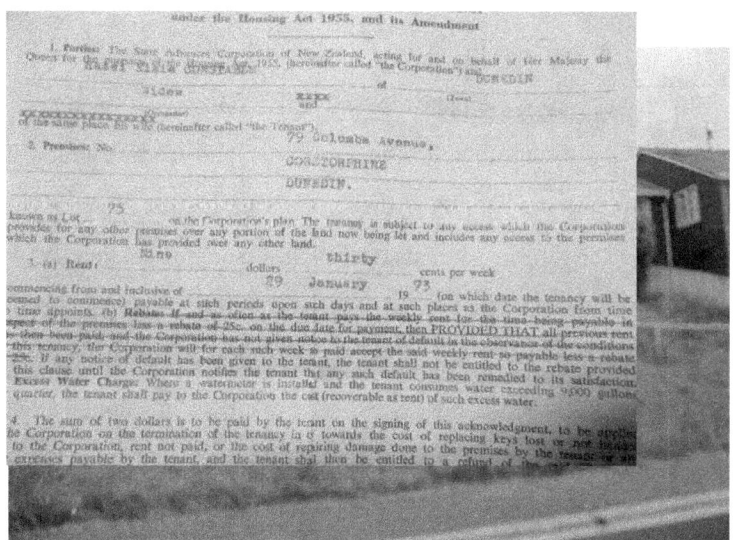

(One of the Didham's trucks on display at Toitu Otago Settlers Museum)

A few months after we moved in, my mother saw an advertisement in the paper for a family needing a babysitter for their two preschool aged sons, Grant (3), and Aaron (9 months). Mum rang up and spoke to the lady about the job. Mum was keen for me to get the work because I would have to give her the money, so it was financially beneficial in this situation, for me to have that freedom. I was more than happy to take it on because it gave me a few hours a week where I could be in someone else's home, in a more normal environment, away from Mum. When the lady found out that we lived across the road and she was the cousin of my Aunty Lorna, she said I could have the job, and asked Mum to send me over so I could meet the children.

When I went over to meet the family, I was told that I could help myself to any food in the house, and I could use the phone once the children went to sleep. She asked if I had a boyfriend. I did, but I couldn't admit to it since I knew she was in contact with Mum. "No," I lied. She said if that changes, you are not allowed to bring the boy over to the house. "You are supposed to be looking after the kids," she said. I agreed.

Jenny worked as a cleaner from 5pm till 7pm Monday to Friday, for extra money for the house. Her husband worked full-time as a coalman, delivering coal to houses to burn in fireplaces. When I came in everyday at 4 pm, Jenny had given the boys their tea and left dessert in the oven for me to serve. Grant was already in his pyjamas when I arrived, but Aaron would need his nappy changed and his pyjamas put on for bed. I put Grant to bed, and Aaron into his cot with a bottle. Once they were both asleep, I then took out all my homework. The homework load at the time was heavy, as I was in the middle of my school certificate year.

Jenny always arrived home first at around 7pm, at which point I was free to go home. After I had been there around three months, Jenny's husband started sneaking home earlier than her. Several times, he came home and found me sitting on the couch. He took a seat very close to me and put his hand on my knee while he talked. He asked me questions about school and what subjects I was taking and made conversation until either Jenny came home or I'd excuse myself, since the babysitter wasn't needed now that the boy's father was home. If we were interrupted by Jenny's arrival, he would shoot up from the couch when he heard her key turn in the door, and stand there chatting, as if he had just walked in himself.

One night, during our chats, he asked me if I had ever kissed anybody. When I said no, he said "Oh...sweet sixteen and never been kissed." I didn't know what to say, so I quickly packed up my belongings and left for home. At the time, it didn't really register that this wasn't an appropriate conversation for us to be having. I didn't think that the situation would escalate beyond that. I was wrong.

One night he came and sat with me and put his hand on my leg and told me that I had a 'really pretty mouth'. After that I started chaining the door, so that he couldn't walk in and sit down. I also changed the way I studied while I was there. Initially I would wait till the boys were in bed and spread out all of my books into piles, organising my subjects over the carpet in order of priority, so that I could get as much study done as possible. Instead, I now kept all of my materials inside my bag apart from the ones I was working on. When I heard him trying to open the door, the chain would catch, and I would quickly pack up my things and unlock the door, walking out past him, as he came in. I didn't want to give him the opportunity to sit with me or catch me off guard. The next few times he came home, he asked if I could come back in to chat, but I said I had to go home and left abruptly.

After a while, he stopped coming home early. Things went back to normal, and I was relieved of my duties by Jenny, who was home first, like she used to be. I felt comfortable again and stopped putting the chain on.

On the last Friday night, I worked there, I had only been babysitting for an hour when he turned up home. He walked in and sat down on the couch next to me but didn't touch me. He looked at me and said,

"I've been coming home early to watch you through the window."

My mind raced, as I tried to remember if I had been doing anything I shouldn't have been. Had I been touching their things, or eating something I shouldn't have been? As I gathered my thoughts, I realised that the house was sitting atop a basement, sitting high off the ground, making it impossible to see into the windows without using a large fireman's ladder. I wasn't sure what he was getting at, or why he would feel the need to stand atop a ladder to watch me. I didn't say anything. I didn't know what to say.

"I've been watching you having sex with your boyfriend."

I didn't understand what he was talking about. My boyfriend had never come to the house, and even if he had, it was impossible to see inside the house from the outside.

"He's a lucky boy. I wish I could have sex with someone like you."

I was in shock and didn't know what to say. I picked up my bag and ran out the door, crying all the way home. When I got home, I didn't know what to do, because I couldn't say anything to Mum. Since it was a Friday, I had the whole weekend to sort out how I was going to handle the situation, since I wasn't due to go back until Monday.

Anytime I came across unwanted advances from men, I could never tell Mum, because I knew she would say that it was all my fault. One night a man on a motorbike pulled up alongside me in the dark, when Mum had sent me to post a letter. He grabbed me by the wrist, and a physical altercation ensued. He had a tan helmet, which was missing the face visor. He was about 40 years old, with a pug nose. I screamed, but nobody heard me. I managed to get away and hid behind a hedge while I watched him searching up and down the street for me. I was 11 years old.

When he finally gave up looking and left, I ran home. I came in the door flushed, and Mum asked me what was wrong. I knew if I told her, that she would say I was walking provocatively or something - that I had somehow caused this. I would then be punished for the part that I played in it. So, I told her I had bumped into a friend, and had to run home because I was aware that I was going to be home later than she would expect. I still remember that man's face to this day.

As a comparison, my friend Janis down the road was approached in prospect park, while she was sitting on a swing. A man came up and exposed himself to her. She ran home and told her mother, and the police were called.

I thought all Saturday about what I could say to get out of the job. If I told my mother what happened I knew that she would have told me my behaviour provoked it, and that the situation was somehow my fault. I had never been able to talk to her about anything because she would have alleged that I flirted with him, "threw my legs around" and brought out what she called my "slutty behaviour". I must have encouraged him in some way - Mum would never think anything else. By Sunday I had decided that I could not go back the next day, because it would surely result in my being raped. I told Mum that my school workload had become too heavy, and I wasn't getting enough homework hours in, with the babysitting job. After all, it was a school cert year. She didn't question my story, but instead tried to encourage me to go back. I said I couldn't keep up the load and that I wouldn't be returning on Monday, so Mum agreed to call Jenny and tell her.

While most young women have these kinds of unfortunate encounters, it was all the more difficult for me to navigate them, due to the fact that I couldn't discuss them with my mother. Of course, these difficulties also took place amongst all of the background problems that I was having at home. While being a teenager is never easy, there was no safe space for me to discuss things that I went through. This naturally had an impact on my mental health.

Carolyn lived over in Panmure Ave. About once a month she would call my mother on a Saturday morning and ask if I could babysit that night. Carolyn and her husband had two little girls, who were always in bed when I got there. I never really saw them, as my job was just to check them while they were asleep. I spent the evening in the lounge watching T.V., doing homework, and talking to friends on the phone. When they came home at midnight, Carolyn's fiancé would then drive me home, without any issues. We used to chat on the way home. He would ask about what subjects I was taking at school, and other small talk. I never felt like I wasn't safe.

Being Brethren

I only spent nine months living at the Columba ave house, but the time that I spent there has never left me. Though by this point in my life, we had moved several times, and lived in different areas of Dunedin, this particular move signalled a sharp shift in my relationship with Mum. A lot of the problems that I had experienced with Mum were building and escalating around the time of us moving into the new property.

At our old house, we attended the Kaikorai Chapel on a Sunday. At Columba Ave, we would walk to the Riselaw Road Chapel on a Sunday morning, for their weekly service. Mum was pleased with this new house because it was within walking distance of a brethren chapel, and she still did not drive. Whilst we were at church one morning, a girl around my age named Christine, asked if I would like to join the Sunday night Bible class. Christine and her father would pick me up at 6:45 in the evening, and bring me home after the Bible study finished at 9pm. All the girls at Bible class were wearing makeup and nice clothes, but I was not allowed to wear either of these things. Despite this, I enjoyed attending because it got me out of the house and away from Mum for a couple of hours a week and having conversations with like-minded teenagers my own age. I got to participate in the group four times, before things went sour.

One Sunday morning, after I had been attending the Bible class for about a month, a boy that I knew from the Bible study group came over to talk to me. He didn't come over to talk about anything specific, but just to make small talk with someone he knew attended the same Bible study, as we were in the same age group. Mum was away chatting to a lady across the room but spotted the boy talking to me. When we got home, she slapped me across the face, and said I was forbidden to go back to the Bible class. She rang Christine's father, and said that I would not be attending anymore, and that he was not to pick me up for future Bible study evenings. I went straight to my room and cried all night. I didn't feel that I had done anything wrong, and I was upset that I couldn't attend anymore. It was another way in which Mum isolated me from others, and from experiences outside of our house.

Shortly after this, Mum signed me into the psychiatric ward at Wakari Hospital—ward eight. All the teenagers in there were drinking, smoking, taking drugs or running away. Since I hadn't done any of these things, I didn't understand why I was admitted there. I felt different to those around me. I came to suspect that she had lied to my psychologist as I was there for two weeks. It was a godsend actually— it gave me space away from her, and the cruel words she continually directed at me—and I enjoyed the company of people my own age.

A tall boy with ginger curly hair used to pass my door on the way to the lunchroom every day. I would say "Hi", and he would politely say "Hi" back, but we never actually took the conversation any further. I remember over the years seeing him working on the roads and remembered him. When we were 40, we met again in a theatrical group called 'The Palladium Players' and we fell in love and went on to marry. Ironically at the time I had just bought a house at 8 Felix St, North East Valley. The house used to be his grandmothers. It felt very serendipitous.

I was not allowed to shut my bedroom door, in any house that we lived in. It was to be left open at all times. I'm not sure what she thought I would get up to.

When we moved to Columba Ave, we were told that redecorators would be coming in a few weeks. Mum decided not to put up our beds until the redecorators came, since we had wire bed bases that needed tools to set them up. Mum said we would have to sleep on a double mattress on the floor in my room. In all the time that I lived there with her, the redecorators never came, and we slept together, on the floor. She told my sister-in-law that she wouldn't let me sleep in a room alone as I might let boys in my window. My room was so high off the ground they would have needed an extension ladder. My sister-in-law Lorraine likened it to Rapunzel as I had really long hair.

For years I had nagged Mum to get my hair cut. The doctor had told her that the length and thickness of my hair was contributing to the ongoing migraines that I suffered from. Because people used to stop us in the street to admire my long hair, and compliment it, I wasn't allowed to have it cut. She enjoyed the attention that my hair provided her. According to Mum, the Bible also said that my hair was my "crowning glory". She was referencing 1 Corinthians 11:15, that states "If a woman has long hair, it is her glory? For long hair is given to her as a covering."

Even though my hair was my "crowning glory" and couldn't be cut for the benefit of my health, it seemed to be acceptable for Mum to pull it out, when she lost her temper. She frequently pulled me around the room by the hair and abused me verbally. I overheard her one day telling my brother Alec "to pull his wife by the hair, because it didn't leave any marks".

I was 16, and not allowed to go out of the house, or wear makeup - not even a bit of lipstick. One Saturday morning, my brother Brian rang Mum. His son Bryan and his daughter Judy wanted to see a movie, but he was busy. He didn't want to drop them off on their own, so Brian asked if he could pick me up and drop the three of us off at the movies and pick us up afterwards. When he arrived, he brought the kids in and Judy was wearing a bit of pink lip gloss. She was nine years old. Mum threw an absolute fit. An argument ensued, and Brian ended up storming out of the house with his two children, and none of us got to go to the movies.

    My school friends used to rush home from school on a Friday night, get changed, put on makeup, and go into town. My life was quite different. Still, at 16, when I got home from school, the door was locked, and the key was put in Mum's apron pocket. Looking at 16-year-olds now, I realise that they appear to be younger than 16 was in the 1970s, when I was 16. At that time, it was not unusual to leave school at 15 and go out into the real world. A lot of people were married at a young age and starting their families. Most of my peers had done a lot of living by the time they were 20. This kind of restrictive environment at home was out of character for that era, and in fact, for any. But it felt especially intense for me, at that time. Mum said that if I was a 'tart' like my school friends, God would punish me. She said that I was 'evil' for wanting to go out with my friends and wanting to wear makeup. If I mentioned boys, I would have gotten a beating. I never mentioned boys ever because I knew how much this would escalate matters further. She would have called me a "trollop". Not being able to socialise was a way for her to further isolate me from others, and was another way in which she could control me.

    As well as all of the physical abuse I have outlined already, Mum also used words as weapons, and as a means of controlling me. By knocking down my confidence, and chipping away at my self-esteem, Mum was attempting to convince me that I would have no life outside of the life that I lived with her. She frequently said things to me like,

> "No-one will ever marry you. You are ugly on the inside and out."

If I tried to push back about any of the things she was saying, or doing to me, I was called "the devil's spawn". This label for me, came out of her deep belief that I was evil, and that any attempts from me to act independently were driven by the devil.

From a young age, it was clear that I had a natural ability to sing. When I sang at home, Mum would quickly interject with a phrase like,

> "I hope you don't think you can sing!"

As I got older, and was wanting to go out with my friends, and striving for a bit of independence, Mum would be quick to remind me that my physical appearance was, in her opinion, substandard. If I talked about leaving the house, I would get dragged to the bathroom cabinet mirror by my hair, where she would push my face hard into it.

> "Look at yourself, you ugly huck. You're no good to anybody."

To make sure her comments really cut deep, she would tell me to:

> "Go out to the Andersons Bay cemetery and get in on top of your father."

At age nine, I decided, after finding out what meat was made of, that I didn't want to eat it anymore. I was crazy about animals, and the thought of eating them repulsed me. But my mother kept putting it on my plate, and forcing me to eat it. When I started gagging, and vomiting it back onto my plate, Mum would spoon it back into my mouth. I will never forget having my own vomit spooned into my mouth. She told me that I had a "kink", and that there was something wrong with my mentality. Whilst all parents encourage their children to eat their dinner, and times were perhaps a bit stricter and harder back then, reflecting on it now, I feel that it was just another choice that was taken from me, and another area of my life in which I could not exert any freedoms or personal choices.

As I got older, Mum had to get stricter, to be able to enact the same level of control that she had been able to hold over me when I was younger. In this sense, things escalated as I grew closer to the age of independence. If I had to identify a mother whose character matched that of my mother, I would point to the mother in the Stephen King film *Carrie*. When I first watched the movie, it resonated with me immediately, and I wondered how he knew what had gone on in my home.

    The mother in *Carrie* was fanatically religious, and in the film, these beliefs mixed with her abusive actions towards her daughter, much like the experience I had of my mother. It was difficult for me to reconcile Mum's professed Christianity, with the abusive environment she created throughout my life. As an adult, I have come to understand that the God I know would not condone this behaviour, and that Mum was not living out the Christian principles she claimed to believe in.

    At our house in Maori Hill, Mum kept erratic hours, doing her housework during the night, and sleeping during the day. Once we moved to Columba Ave, Mum started keeping more regular hours. The television network shut down at night after the Alfred Hitchcock Hour screened, after which Mum would do some housework, before coming to bed at midnight. Since she didn't trust me to sleep on my own, Mum used to come and get into bed beside me. Just before I left home, Mum told me that I looked so peaceful when I was asleep, I looked like an angel and that she wished I could stay that way forever. I worried that she was going to put a pillow over my face in my sleep. This affected my ability to sleep during the night. I used to wait to go to sleep until she got into bed with me and fell asleep, because I was worried that she would harm me while I was sleeping.

(This is the only photo I had taken at Columba Ave, since I wasn't there long)

It was Wednesday the 26th of September, 1973. I had told Mum the day before that I was going to the music festival at the Dunedin Town Hall, and she had said I could go. After tea I went and changed. When she saw that I wasn't wearing my uniform, she said I wasn't allowed to go. I had been singing in the festival for the past two years but was not participating this year.

Mum was not aware of this - she thought I was going to sing, when in reality, I was going to support my friends. I was a couple of months shy of turning 17 and still wasn't allowed to go anywhere. So, I pushed back.

"I am going."

She flew off the couch and came at me. She smashed me across the face with her fist, then started pulling me around the room by the hair. While she was dragging me, she started screaming, "Jo, help me!" Jo was the next-door neighbour that she had gone to school with. I'm not sure what she expected her to do, considering she was riddled with arthritis. Mum was ripping chunks out of my scalp, and the struggle went on for around ten minutes. When she grabbed my wrists, I pushed her back and made for the front door. It had a deadlock and a chain, but I managed to get them both undone quickly and ran down the path toward Clorinda's house. I told her parents what had happened, and they let me use the phone to ring my Aunty Daisy. She was disgusted. She told me to go to the music festival as planned, then go back to Clorinda's house and ring her and she would come pick me up from there. To look at Mum you would think 'butter didn't melt in her mouth' but when she was in a rage, she was very strong, and her bodyweight far outweighed that of mine.

I went to the town hall and at halftime when I went to the toilet, I saw Mum in the foyer. She glared at me. I think she was checking I was there and not lying about where I was going. After it finished, we left quickly so as not to encounter her again. We got the bus to Clorinda's house and I rang my Aunty. When she picked me up, she took me down to the central police station, she said if a Hazel Constable rang to report her daughter missing that I was staying with her. She showed them the chunks missing out of my scalp. Today, Mum would have been arrested but back then you could do what you liked to your own kids. The police said that since I was the legal age of 16, they wouldn't make me go home.

By the time I ran away, I had a wee Pomeranian called Kimmy. She was my dog growing up, and she used to know what time I got in from school and would wait at the door. When I ran away, I couldn't take her. Mum told my sister-in-law that Kimmy waited at the door at the same time every day for weeks, when I was due home from school.

The next day, I had a really bad headache, so stayed in bed all day. A couple of days later, Aunty Daisy made an appointment to see the principal, Miss Upchurch, she explained it all to her and asked if there was a uniform, I could borrow to see out the year, all I had was the clothes on my back. She gave me a uniform that I had to return when I finished with it, and I went to school the next day. My brother Brian went to see Mum and asked if I could have some clothes which he brought to me, he stayed for tea and they talked about Mum, how she needed to go back in for treatment, but they didn't think she would agree. By then you couldn't sign someone into a mental health facility, they had to go of their own free will.

Looking back, I now think that Mum had a touch of Munchausen Syndrome by proxy (MSP) This is now referred to as Factitious Disorder imposed on another (FDIA). This mental illness involves a person acting as if their child, or someone in their life that they care for, is sick when they are not. Some people may recognise this illness from the famous case of Gypsy Rose, whose life was made into a Netflix limited series *The Act*. While my mother did not take the illness as far, or to the same degree of severity, I do see facets of that illness when I remember some of her behaviour around my health.

Mum had an obsession with doctors and nurses. I think it was because they paid her attention. She used to get crushes on her Drs and knit them Aran jerseys. I thought the fact that they accepted them was weird and unprofessional. As a child she used to make up things about me to get x-rays and tests done to get attention for herself. She took me regularly to a Dr called Mr Horowitz to get my ears syringed with hot water. I hated it. Although he used to let me have a blackball from his jar afterwards, which made it somewhat more pleasant. She used to take me to a psychiatrist and tell them things that I hadn't done -

things that she herself had said. She used to say to me that she was worried that someone would break in and stab her. She told the doctors that I was worried someone would stab me. I had not said this. When I was young, they used to speak to me with her in the room, so there was no opportunity for me to correct this. When I was still living at home, one of the psychiatrist's asked to speak to me alone. His name was Jonathon McLeod and his rooms were in George St, just past Frederick St. It was an old building with a highly polished staircase, and it smelled of leather. He was on the top floor. After that I used to go and see him after school. One day he asked me why I hid behind my hair. My hair was very long with a middle part, as was fashionable in the seventies. I used to leave it forward, hanging, and peek out at him from the side. He tried to reassure me and get me to open up.

> "This is a safe place. Pull your hair back and let's have a face-to-face chat."

After that, I used to go with my hair tied back. I confided in him what was going on at home. He was very sympathetic. He said he wouldn't disclose the information if I didn't want him to, and I agreed that it was best kept between us. After I ran away from home, I went to see him one more time. He said he didn't need to see me anymore, as I was out of "that awful situation". I told him

I was finally free. I think speaking to him partly gave me the confidence to leave, which is why I have always remembered his name.

Young Love and Finally Breaking Free

This particular time in my life would bring me joy—in the form of young love, but it also represents my first step out of my mother's shadow, and into freedom. These two paradigms became entwined with each other, as I fought to make a life for myself, and finally separate myself from Mum.

I started school at the end of January in my sixth form year (now referred to as year 12) from our house at Columba Ave, Lookout Point. I only passed one subject in the fifth form - home economics, so I had to resist. Standing at the bus stop one morning, another girl from my school, Otago Girls High, was smiling at me. She was very pretty, and I smiled back, but we didn't speak till a few days later. She came over to me and said her name was Clorinda and asked what mine was. She was in the third form but seemed very mature for her age. We clicked right away, and she became my best friend.

One day, we got on the bus and sat at the back. She introduced me to a few of her friends, which included a boy named Gordon. It was love at first sight, and I will never forget those big brown sparkly eyes, and that lovely curly black hair. He smiled at me with a smile that gave me goosebumps.

The next morning on the bus, he came and sat down beside me, and started asking me about myself. One thing led to another, and we ended up seeing each other.

I had been meeting another boy called Chris at lunchtimes sometimes, but he sent me a note this particular day, saying he couldn't meet me. That's where it ended, as far as I can remember. I was friends with Chris's sister Sue, we sat beside each other in class. Sue took home a class photo that we had had taken and Chris asked who the pretty girl was, it was me. The next day he sent along a note for me, and we used to meet sometimes at lunchtime up at the observatory as he went to Otago Boys High school. He was a nice boy with cool hair and reminded me of the surfies in the television show *Gidget*. I've never forgotten him, nor he, I, and to this day, we remain good friends.

Gordon and I were inseparable and would meet at lunchtimes every day at Kensington Station. I would bus there, and he would walk as it was halfway between the two schools. I would often get there first and when I saw him coming up the steps my heart would melt. We also met for an hour every day after school. Often, we would sit in a little alcove in the Dowling st steps. We would talk, laugh, kiss, hug, and sometimes I would sing to him from my song books.

Mum used to send me to the shop for a newspaper on a Saturday night, and he would be waiting for me outside the store. Stolen moments, as I wasn't allowed out. I'll never forget the sight of him, standing there, waiting. My heart used to skip a beat. Faded blue jeans, a sweater, and a school scarf around his neck. If Mum had found out I had a boyfriend, I would have got a hell of a hiding.

We were together most of that year, and sometimes I would go to his house after school. He had a room under the house that had been converted from the basement. You had to go around the back of the house to access it, and he shared it with his brother Peter. We headed straight down there when I arrived, but then his mother would call us up and make us sit in the kitchen

We only ever kissed, nothing more, but if Mum had found out, she would have accused me of having sex. Her mind always went to that.

We used to skip school sometimes, so we could spend the whole day together. We would go out to Brighton on the bus to visit my friend Anne who was now married with a baby and sit on the beach or we would sit in the waiting room at the railway station.

I bought him a friendship ring - something you did in those days if you were dating. We talked about getting married, but he was younger than me, so I knew it wouldn't be happening anytime soon.

Gordon was a boxer, and he used to go out of town on the bus to matches for Coster's Gym sometimes on the weekends. I used to hate those Saturday nights when he wasn't waiting for me at the shop.

Once a month on a Saturday, I collected the subscription fees for the Otago Daily Times. I had to go door to door and collect the payments. I'd have breakfast, and then head out. By the time I got home, it was getting dark. It was made more time consuming by the chit chat that the older ladies wanted to have, and sometimes they weren't prepared to make all the payment and needed some time to count the payment. I had to write down how much they had paid and get the client to sign their book. If they didn't have enough money to pay the whole month, then their bill was carried over to the following month. When my boyfriend Gordon didn't have boxing, he sometimes came with me, although Mum didn't know about this. At lunchtime we would go and get something from the dairy and sneak into the Gazebo at 'Corstorphine House' to eat it. It was private property and we weren't supposed to be there but we never got caught. I love gazebos and have always wanted one.

On Monday morning, the man would come around to the house and collect the money bag from Mum. I would deduct my wages from the bag and give him the rest. It paid well, but the best part about the job was getting away from Mum for the day.

When we were sitting at the bus shed one day, at Lookout Point, my cousin who was a bus driver, spotted us, and told his mother - my mother's older sister. She rang and told Mum. I don't know how she found out his name, but my mother looked Gordon's family up in the phonebook and called his mother. Mum told Gordon's mother that I was a bisexual, and that I had a venereal disease (STD). After that, his mother didn't like me very much, and tried to discourage him from seeing me. Mum was always very convincing with her lies. She also started ringing Clorinda's mother, telling her that we were in a lesbian relationship with each other, and that she was worried that there would be another 'Parker-Hulme type case' involving us.

After I ran away from home, Mum continued to call Clorinda's mother, filling her head with lies about me. Eventually Clorinda's mother stopped me from going to their house anymore. Before that, we used to have sleepovers. Mum tried to destroy every relationship I ever had with anyone.

When I ran away from home, I was living with my Aunty Daisy at Appold St, Mornington.

(Daisy Stephens when she was younger)

After running away, I hadn't seen Gordon for three days, because I hadn't been attending school. I was in a lot of pain, and I still had patches from my scalp missing, from the events of that night.

My brother Brian arranged to pick Gordon up and bring him up to see me. Brian stayed and had a cup of tea with Aunty Daisy and Uncle Herbert, while Gordon and I went for a walk. Gordon told me he loved me every day, and when we put his arms around me, I felt special, and loved. No one had ever cuddled me since my dad. Mum said no boy would ever want me, because I was ugly on the inside, and out.

I ran away on the 26th of September 1973. On the 10th of October, at 8 o'clock at night, my Aunty Daisy called me to the phone. She said it wasn't Gordon, but that it was another boy. It was Paul, one of Gordon's friends, who lived down at the Point. He said that Gordon wanted to break up with me. I asked if Gordon was there, and Paul said that Gordon did not want to speak with me. I hung up the phone, not really understanding what was going on. Clorinda rang me straight after and said she had heard them talking about it outside her house.

I was devastated. We were in love, or so I thought. He didn't even have the courage to tell me himself. I cried for days - didn't sleep or eat, didn't go to school. My Aunty would bring in cups of tea. One day, my Aunty came in and said that I had to go back to school, so I decided to go and wait at the school gate for him, when school would be due out. He didn't want to speak to me. To this day, I don't know what went wrong, and having spoken to him as an adult, he doesn't remember either. Pressure from his parents, and his best friend who didn't like me, was possibly the cause. I often wonder if I hadn't run away from home if things would have stayed the same. I guess he got used to not seeing me every day, and it gave him time to think. I went home that night, went into my Aunty's medicine cabinet, and took a whole bottle of aspirin. The next thing I remember, was finding myself in the hospital having my stomach pumped. What a dreadful experience.

I'm so thankful I didn't die that night at 16. My three children wouldn't be here, and I wouldn't have experienced everything in life that I have. But, at the time, I couldn't think of being here without him. The only person who ever loved me, no longer did, and I couldn't see any future. If you watch the movie 'Splendour in the Grass', the character of Deanie was me after we broke up.

(Gordon)

(Gordon's house at 55 Riselaw Road, Lookout Point)

After that my Aunty Daisy rang my brother and told him that he'd have to find somewhere else for me to stay because I wasn't getting on with my grumpy uncle. He picked at me the whole time, and he was much older than my Aunty.

I packed my clothes and Brian came to pick me up. I was going to live with my brother Alec and his wife Loraine in Archibald st, Waverley. I just had a mattress on the floor between two of my nephews' beds, so it wasn't ideal. While I was living there, my friend Madelon came to school with this new 'pageboy' haircut. I loved it and had been wanting to cut my hair since I left home, so I went home and asked my sister-in-law Loraine if I could have some money to get my haircut. The next day Madelon took me down to the hairdresser where she got hers done, we had to get the bus at lunchtime, it was way down the north end of George st, past the Cherry Court Lodge. They did my hair exactly the same and gave me what they had cut off in a plastic bag, it was really long. Sadly when I left home the second time, mum kept it. It wasn't there when we cleaned out her house when she went into a rest home, so I'm guessing she sold it to a wigmaker.

    I finished school in November and got a job at Arthur Barnett's in the wool department. By then Lorraine had asked me to leave too because I wasn't getting on with my oldest nephew. He kept kicking my legs under the tea table and laughing about it, and really there wasn't any room for me. My other brother Eddie lived up the road and had a spare room, but it never occurred to me to ask if I could stay there. This might have been better, since they had no children at that time.

    So, I went to live with my brother Brian at Woodside, Outram. He had a partner named Bunny by this time, and custody of two of his children, aged 12 and 9. Bunny was of Maori descent, and in her 30s. I shared a room with my nine-year-old niece, Judy. Brian had a ute and the cab only had three seats. When we went out, he put us kids in the back of the ute and covered us up with a dome canvas cover. When we went over Three-Mile-Hill, we all used to roll into each other, which we used to giggle about. It was highly illegal. If we'd gone over the edge, we'd all have been killed.

Brian was separated from his wife Mary, but there was no legal custody arrangement for the children. Only two of the four were at school, the other two were too young. Mary was living in Christchurch. Brian found out which school the two older children went to and went and picked them up. He told the Police he had them. He never got the other two, so they were raised separately.

Gordon started coming to see me on a Friday night with a school friend. He would come into Arthur Barnett's and talk to me at the counter while I worked. Eventually he asked for my number and started calling me. We used to talk on the phone for a couple of hours, but neither one said anything about getting back together. He probably assumed I would react negatively to this, and I assumed the same. To get to work in the morning, I had to get on the 7am bus which passed our house. The bus then took us to the train, where we got off and took the train into central Dunedin. The last bus going back to Outram was at teatime, and my shift ended at 9pm. I couldn't suggest a meet up with Gordon, as Brian used to make me be at the car by 9.15pm, or he would leave without me. I had to run from my 9pm finish to get straight to Brian's car before he left me behind. He closed his second-hand shop called Woodside Traders in Rattray st at 9pm. On weekdays, he closed his shop at 5:30. I finished work at 5:30, so he would give me 15 minutes to get down to Rattray st. When I was working at Arthur Barnett's, I made good friends with a girl called Robyn Brown at the record counter. I started spending the weekend at her house, so I didn't have to run to Brian's car. She lived in Taieri road, and she had a lovely mum.

One night he did leave without me, so I rang my friend Robyn and she said I could get the bus to her house. He was my only transport to Outram, at that late hour, so Gordon and I were restricted to phone conversations. I didn't want to get hurt again by suggesting we resume our relationship, and so many things were left unsaid. I regret not having said anything as I've never loved anyone as deeply as I loved him. A part of me still does. They say, 'the first cut is the deepest', and it's true.

Mum got me fired from my position at Arthur Barnett's. She started coming in, sitting on the chair beside my counter, talking to me while I served customers. Mum kept telling me that she had renovated my bedroom, painting my furniture in purple and white because it was my favourite colour. She had purchased curtains with a purple fleck in them and chose a wallpaper that had a lavender fleur de lis pattern on it. She promised that if I came back home, things would be different. I was working now, and an adult, so I would be treated with all the freedoms of one. She would stay for hours, in plain sight of the managers who were watching the counter from the next floor.

They called me in for a meeting and asked who the woman was that kept sitting at the counter for hours. I was served a written warning and told me that I needed to ask her not to come in. When she came in next time, I told her that her presence was getting me into trouble, but she persisted in coming in about twice a week and sitting at my counter for about three hours. About three weeks after my written warning, I was called into the managerial office again. This time, they let me go.

I went home to Brian's, and I was scared. Even though it wasn't my fault, I thought Brian would likely give me a hiding for it. I told his partner Bunny that I had been let go, and that I feared Brian's reaction. She advised that I get another job ASAP, before Brian could find out that I was out of work. Bunny was very protective of me. Brian slapped me once, in the face, while I was living there, and Bunny told him he was not allowed to do that again. On Monday, at lunchtime, I walked into Haywright's and asked about a position there. I was hired on the spot for their haberdashery department, and evaded Brian's wrath. I went home and told Brian that I was going to approach Haywright's about a job because I was tired of my job at Arthur Barnett's. He said it was fine with him, as long as I had a job to go to. He never found out that there was ever a time where I was between jobs.

When I stayed at Robyn's house, we used to go to Moana Pool. One time, I met a friend of hers there, called Bruce.

Bruce was at Moana pool with his cousin Warren. Robyn knew all the 'Halfway Bush boys', or so she called them. She was dating Greg, who got round with David, Bruce, Warren, and Keith. Robyn introduced me to Bruce, who kept staring at me. Bruce was older than me and had thick auburn hair. He was about 5'9" and had a light, freckled complexion. He was very quiet, but friendly.

Because I was stuck out in Outram with no transport, Bruce's car, and his ability to drive was very appealing. Robyn suggested that Bruce give me a ride home from the pool and we chatted all the way to Outram. He told me about his home life, and how he was raising his little brother after his father had thrown his mother out of the house. His father was never home, and so it was just the two of them. When he dropped me off, he asked if he could see me again. I said he could pick me up from work the next day, and it started from there. The instant attraction that I had with Gordon was missing, but as things developed, we became fond of each other.

While I was dating Bruce, and he was bringing me home from work every night, Bunny left Brian because of his abuse towards her. I came home and found that she had moved out, and I was scared. Bunny had been my protector while I lived with him, and now she was gone. I recalled the promises that Mum had made in Arthur Barnett's. If I came back home, things would be different. I believed her.

I threw all of my stuff in the back of Bruce's car and told him that I would have to go back home. He drove me there, but I was only there for a few weeks. When Bruce used to come to pick me up, Mum would yell things out the window, to try and put him off me.

"You know she used to be a lesbian!"

"She has VD!"

"She was born deaf in the right ear; it could be hereditary!".

Things were getting bad again and I wasn't having the freedom she promised, she started locking the back door when I got in from work.

She used to ring my Aunt Phyllis and tell lies about me. One night I walked into the kitchen to find Mum and Phyllis. Aunty Phyllis slapped me in the face. Mum made up a story after that night and spread it around the family. She said that I pushed Aunty Phyllis that night, in response to her slapping me. I loved and respected her, I would never do that. According to Mum's story, Phyllis hit her head on the cupboard. A few years later Phyllis had an aneurysm, and Mum blamed me for it, when she was talking to family. Phyllis' unfortunate aneurysm fit conveniently into Mum's story, and she took full advantage of it.

When I went to visit her in the hospital, the doctor told me that an artery in her brain had become brittle from years of smoking. At the time of the aneurysm, this artery burst open and caused the bleed. She was in a coma for months, and never came out. She eventually passed away.

When I had moved back home, Mum used to scan the newspapers for funeral notices, to see if she had the slightest connection to anyone. If she did, she would note down the day and time of the funeral, with a plan to go. For example, if a childhood friend's cousin had died, she would attend the funeral. My brother Alec nicknamed her, "the professional mourner", and thought that perhaps she was going for the free food she could eat while she was there. In addition, she would wrap up sandwiches, and savouries in serviettes. She would leave with a handbag full of leftovers to enjoy later that night. I thought that she enjoyed going because she would get to be around a lot of people, and her presence there would bring her attention.

When I ran away from home the final time, I was working at Haywright's. I went to live with my friend Margaret in Salmond st. Her Mum had five children and they were moving to a bigger house. When I was eating my tea one night, she came out and said there wasn't going to be any room at the new house, and that I would need to put an advertisement in the paper to find a private board. I put an advertisement in 'the evening star'. The only answer I got was a lady called Lorraine C in Brockville, so I moved in there. I quickly became good friends with her 11-year-old daughter, Ginny (Virginia Ann Kahui). Ginny was mature for her age. Her Mother had entrusted her with a lot of the child raising responsibilities, while she worked.

While I was living with Lorraine C, Bruce and I got engaged. We got married and I gave birth to a baby boy. The marriage only lasted a few years, we both brought excess baggage into the relationship from our dysfunctional childhoods, I came from a childhood that allowed me no freedom, into marriage and after a while I felt trapped. When we went to the Nees Ball, I was introduced as Mrs Bruce Sparks, a thing they did in those days. This made me uncomfortable, and led me to question my identity? I'd lost it and I yearned to have freedom.

We got divorced, and I was single from my mid to late 20s. It was the 80s, and I had a good time going out with my friends.

When I was 30, I married again to a controlling abusive man whom I stayed with for 11 years, but that's a whole other story.

Epilogue

When I look in the mirror, now that I'm older, I look more like my mother than my father. It's just a daily reminder of what I endured growing up and I don't like what I see. Maybe God is trying to tell me something-that she was my mother, and it's time to let go of the past. The bad times outweighed the good, but there were a few good and sometimes I miss those times. Even though she wasn't really a mother to me, sometimes I miss her. I never got an apology, she was in denial. Later in life, when I tried to raise some of these memories with her, in an attempt to have a conversation and try and resolve them, Mum didn't remember the events—or chose not to.

Mum died in 2001, 20 years ago. I feel like it must be time to forgive and forget now and be at peace for when my time comes.

(Mum, around the age I am now)

Afterword

The effects of my time with my mother have had lasting effects on my life. It has made me emotionally fragile, and it doesn't take much to make me cry. Because abuse had been normalised in my childhood home, I also allowed it to seep into my adult life, marrying a man who abused me, and accepting that this too was normal. Years of being crushed and devalued by Mum's words over me also contributed to my own feelings of worthlessness in my romantic relationships and knocked my confidence in many areas of life.

I first thought about writing this book in my 50s, several years after Mum died. As I was busy, and still raising my youngest child, it slid to the bottom of the 'to do' list, and as a result, has been a long project in the making.

I started writing it when I was 60, when my time allowed it. By this time in my life, I had retired, and I had more time not just to write, but also to deal with the emotional load that I knew this project would draw. I think in the back of my mind, I had delayed starting, because I was acutely aware of how difficult it was going to be to relive all of these memories and articulate them in my own words.

Because I hadn't dealt properly with some of these events—and had not even shared some of them before the publication of this book—it seemed like a door that I may not want to open. I knew that letting these experiences seep back into my life was going to be painful and would challenge me in ways that I had not been ready to cope with before. Because I had not revealed some of the more severe recollections with even my children, it also seemed like I would have to include them in the journey I was about to take.

Even though I delayed the process until I felt I was ready to do this, putting my story down in words was even more painful than I had anticipated. It's taken me five years to piece together this memoir. At times it was easier, especially when I got to relive my time with Dad and write about the happy years that we spent together. At other times, when I was struggling with the particularly difficult material, the book was put aside for a few months and then picked up again, when I felt like I was in a more robust emotional position to tackle it once more.

While this project took more years, and more emotional energy, than I expected it to, I am pleased to be on the other side of it and wrapping up this journey. While most of the problems that existed in my relationship with Mum will go on unresolved, I think it has been beneficial for my own growth, to be able to reflect on the events in my younger life, and at least find some closure. Though I can never fully close the door on my childhood, where I lived in my mother's shadow, I feel that in writing this book, I have been able to bring out these experiences into the light.

Credits

p. 24.
Dictionary of New Zealand, "Biography Volume Two (1870-1900)". Accessed online:
http://www.dnzb.govt.nz/dnzb/default.asp?Find_Quick.asp?PersonEssay=2L5

p. 27.
Otago Daily Times, "Patients died locked in rooms", 27 Jan 2018, Accessed online:
https://www.odt.co.nz/news/dunedin/patients-died-locked-rooms

p. 36.
Adriaan de Winter and Ton van Alphen

P. 40.
Otago Daily Times: Evening Star

p. 84.
Judy Constable (Brian)
Marlene Fahey (nee Baker) (Alec)

p. 91.
Museum of New Zealand Te Papa Tongarewa

p. 133
"Maori Hill Store and Fisher's Meats Butchery", Highgate c1970s, *DCC Archives*, Photo Box B/47B. Accessed online:
https://www.flickr.com/photos/dccarchives/24851283952/in/photolist-EbEwPq-EAtkM9-DS2jUY-Hig4qa-DAkxQ5-24v3cux-omg71T-okHm3C

"Maori Hill Shops, c1978"
DCC Archives, Planning Series, Negative Sheet 12/22.
Accessed online:
https://www.flickr.com/photos/dccarchives/40366370115/in/photolist-EbEwPq-EAtkM9-DS2jUY-Hig4qa-DAkxQ5-24v3cux-omg71T-okHm3C

p. 147
"Frederick Street Conveniences, 1975"
City Architects Photo Album 'Parks and Recreation Toilets, etc, 2 (1967-87)', *DCC Archives*
Accessed online:
https://www.flickr.com/photos/dccarchives/49010079821

p. 176.
"George Street c1977"
DCC Archives, Planning Department 'Views over CBD Album'
Accessed online:
https://www.flickr.com/photos/dccarchives/49852032618

p. 181.
Madelon White (nee Janssen)

p. 190.
Toitū Otago Settlers Museum